THAI

HOW TO THINK, MOVE, AND DOMINATE LIKE THE APEX PREDATOR IN BUSINESS.

TIGER

NIM STANT

Cover design by International Impact Book Awards
Interior design and formatting by International Impact Book Awards

Hardcover ISBN: 979-8-9931138-0-7
Published by Nim Stant
For more information, visit *ThaiTiger.com*

First Edition
2025

CONTENTS

INTRODUCTION   BORN WILD, BUILT FOR THE   11
                 JUNGLE

CHAPTER 1   THE JUNGLE IS REAL   17

CHAPTER 2   TERRITORY ISN'T GIVEN — IT'S   29
                 TAKEN

CHAPTER 3   KILL THE NICE GIRL   41

CHAPTER 4   EYES ON THE TARGET   55

CHAPTER 5   THE SOLO HUNT   67

CHAPTER 6   BITE DOWN. STRIKE FAST.   79

CHAPTER 7   PROWL QUIETLY. MOVE   89
                 PUBLICLY.

CHAPTER 8   DON'T EAT WHAT YOU KILL   101

CHAPTER 9   THE TIGER WAY   113

CHAPTER 10   PROTECT THE FIRE   125

CHAPTER 11   THERE'S BLOOD ON THE THRONE   135

CHAPTER 12   DISRUPT THE GAME, DON'T JUST   149
                PLAY IT

CHAPTER 13   MONEY IS THE MEGAPHONE   165

CHAPTER 14   LIGHT THE FIRE, BURN THE MAP   179

CHAPTER 15   EYES ON YOU   197

ABOUT THE   NIM STANT   209
AUTHOR

INTRODUCTION

BORN WILD, BUILT FOR THE JUNGLE

The world is a jungle. Not just metaphorically—but viscerally. Sharp. Fast. Unforgiving. The moment you hesitate, something hungrier takes your spot. And the business world? It's a jungle dressed in suits and smiles. Wolves in sheep's clothing. Fake support. Empty praise. It'll clap for you on Monday and undercut you on Tuesday. If you don't know who you are, it will tell you. And the story it writes won't be in your favor.

I didn't grow up in the jungle of Wall Street or Silicon Valley. I grew up in the real jungle: Thailand, where I learned to survive before I ever learned to speak up. Where the heat makes you strong and the struggle makes you smart. Where you don't wait for opportunity—you make it. I didn't grow up dreaming of becoming a CEO. I grew up dreaming of having enough. Enough food. Enough freedom. Enough voice to say yes without asking anyone's permission.

At twenty-one, I left my home with nothing but a backpack, a deep hunger, and one irrational belief—that maybe, just maybe, I was made for something more. I didn't know any English. I had no roadmap. No backup plan. Just instinct. Like a tiger forced into new terrain, I had to find my footing fast.

Then life hit harder. I became a solo mom of two, teaching yoga in five studios a day. I was waking up in the dark and falling asleep in tears. I drove across town in a beat-up car, smiling for students while breaking quietly inside. Most days, I was scraping together gas money and praying my kids didn't feel the fear I was swallowing just to get through another week. But I kept going. Not because I had strength—but because I didn't have a choice.

That's what this book is. Not a business manual. Not a highlight reel. This is survival. Power. Strategy. Wild instinct. This is the truth no one posts on Instagram.

Because the jungle doesn't care about your résumé—it cares if you move. If you adapt. If you strike fast enough, the world can't put you in a cage.

You don't win out here by being fearless. You win by being feral. Precise. Focused. Unrelenting.

Tigers don't chase everything—they stalk. They don't roar all day—they strike when it counts. They don't live for approval —they live for dominance. That's how I built my life. That's how I built my brand. That's how I turned struggle into strategy, and pain into power.

Today, I run a global media company. I host red carpet galas. I lead the International Impact Book Awards—and I'm building it to become the Oscars for Authors. But none of this came from being polished. It came from knowing how to move in the jungle—fast, demanding, and real.

If you're tired of being told to "be positive," "be patient," or "play nice," this book is for you. If you've ever felt underestimated, invisible, or tired of waiting your turn… this book is for you. And if you're finally ready to stop asking for permission and start owning the territory you were born for… this book is yours.

This is not about pretending to be fearless. It's about becoming ferocious—even while afraid. You don't need another plan. You need instinct. Precision. Fire. You need to remember who the hell you are.

You're not here to be hunted. You're here to lead. To strike. To rise.

Welcome to the jungle. Now—show them your claws.

- Nim Stant

"The jungle isn't waiting for you to feel ready. It's moving—with or without you."

- Nim Stant

CHAPTER 1

THE JUNGLE IS REAL

THE MOMENT YOU STEP IN, EVERYTHING WANTS TO TEST YOU

The world is a jungle. Life. Business. Every negotiation, every opportunity, every boardroom—it's all survival. And in the jungle, you're either the predator or the prey.

I once sat across from a businessman. He was polished and well-connected. He had been in business longer than I had and exuded the kind of confidence that comes from money and power—but he also gave off the energy that comes from underestimating someone. He talked and talked, bragging about who he knew, what doors he could open for me, and how I'd never make it without him.

I listened. I watched. But I didn't flinch—because I knew exactly what was happening.

He thought I was just another soft-spoken immigrant woman. He thought I'd smile, nod, and say yes to anything just to get ahead. He thought I was a Thai bunny—sweet, quiet, useful.

But I gathered my energy, looked him dead in the eye, and said:

"You think I'm a Thai bunny, don't you? Just so you know —I'm a Thai Tiger."

That was the moment the entire dynamic shifted. The deal was mine—not because I raised my voice or because I overexplained, but because I showed up in my power.

Tigers don't beg. They don't chase. They don't ask for approval. They observe, they decide, and they strike. Alone if necessary. Fearless when it counts. That's what business is. That's what leadership is. That's what survival looks like.

If you're waiting for someone to give you permission, you're not hunting—you're hiding. And no one in the jungle eats by waiting.

The jungle doesn't ask if you're ready. It doesn't care about your excuses. It only asks one question:

Are you built to last?

When I first stepped into the world of business, I didn't walk in with a team behind me. I didn't have capital. I didn't have connections. I had no mentor holding my hand, no investor writing a check, no family legacy to lean on. What I had was hunger, a sharp mind, and claws I hadn't learned to use yet.

People looked at me like I was cute. Ambitious. But unrealistic. I was a single mom, a former yoga teacher with an accent, trying to build something from scratch in a country I didn't even grow up in.

They didn't say it out loud, but I saw it in their eyes: **"Who does she think she is?"**

I'll tell you who I am.

I'm the one who kept building while they whispered.

I'm the one who didn't flinch when the support didn't show up. I'm the one who sharpened my claws in silence until I was ready to strike.

Tigers are not born respected. They earn their power in the wild. Not because someone hands it to them—but because they refuse to die. They don't need the herd. They don't need applause. They survive because they trust their instincts, move with precision, and never beg for safety.

In business, no one is coming to rescue you. There is no perfect plan. No magical moment when everyone suddenly believes in you. You either show up for yourself—or get devoured by someone who's hungrier.

No one believed in me when I started—not really. They were polite and curious, but they weren't betting on me.

That's fine. I wasn't asking for permission.

I was building anyway.

Tigers are solitary by design. They don't move in packs. They don't rely on backup. They don't need a crowd to validate their next move. In the wild, a tiger is built to hunt, survive, and dominate—alone. It stalks with silence, strikes with precision, and disappears without needing applause. It doesn't ask for permission. It doesn't wait for consensus. It knows what it is—and it acts like it.

Entrepreneurs could learn a lot from that. Because in business, too many people waste years waiting. Waiting for the right team, the right partner, the right mentor. Waiting for more clarity, more validation, more green lights. Waiting to be picked. And while they wait, someone else is already making the move. Someone else is claiming the opportunity. Someone else is eating.

Tigers don't wait. They observe, decide, and strike. No pitch deck. No second-guessing. No crowd-sourced opinions. They move—and by the time you realize it, the moment is already theirs. That's what leadership looks like. Not noise, not consensus—action.

If you're building something real, something bold, something that challenges what people think is possible—don't expect a parade. Most of your journey will be lonely. There will be no cheering section at 5:00 AM when you're grinding in silence. No one will be clapping when you double your rates or cut ties with a client who drains you. Most people won't even understand what you're building until it's already built. That's the price of leading.

You have to hold the vision when no one else believes. You have to lead yourself when no one else shows up. You have to decide that your dream is worth moving forward with—even if you're the only one moving. That's tiger energy. Quiet. Powerful. Unapologetic.

The tiger doesn't chase everything. It picks its target. Locks in. And moves. That's how you win in business, too. Not by doing everything. Not by pleasing everyone. But by knowing exactly what you're after—and going for it with discipline and precision.

So, if you're still waiting for the mentor, the map, the momentum, ask yourself this: Are you building a business—or just begging for approval? Stop waiting for someone to walk with you. Stop looking around for signs. You were built to move alone. You were built to hunt.

Be the tiger.

The jungle doesn't hand out welcome signs. It doesn't care if you're scared, talented, or well-intentioned. It doesn't reward effort. It rewards results. In the jungle—as in business—survival is earned, not given.

I was raised in Korat, Thailand. Not in the luxury of the city, but in the kind of upbringing that teaches you early how to read a room, count every dollar, and never waste a move. That was my jungle.

I learned fast that life didn't promise safety. My family didn't have extra. My mom worked hard as an elementary school teacher. We didn't dine out for fun—we ate out when it was necessary. Once, she took us to a restaurant and told us we could each order just one thing. If we were still hungry, we'd eat more at home. I wasn't embarrassed. I was aware. I was watching. I knew from a young age that no one was coming to save me. And survival—my own, my family's, my future—was going to be my responsibility.

Tigers know this, too.

In the wild, a tiger doesn't hunt with reckless energy. It doesn't run around trying to impress other animals. It waits. Watches. Measures. Times. And when the moment is right—it strikes with everything it has. One hit. Clean. Calculated. Strategic.
Do you know what a tiger's success rate is in the wild? Ten percent. That means they fail nine out of ten times. And they still hunt. They still stalk. They still strike.

Why? Because survival isn't about never failing. It's about never stopping.

That lesson saved my life in business.

When I came to the U.S., nobody was betting on me. I had no money. No English skills. No roadmap. I didn't show up with a business degree or a pitch deck. I showed up with fire. That's it.

I took jobs no one wanted. Cleaned floors. Worked in multiple yoga studios a day. Raised two kids solo. I learned business by doing it—failing, bleeding, and adjusting. I had to earn every inch.

There was no strategy book that could teach me what experience and grit did. No one was coming to tell me I was on the right track. So, I did what tigers do—I moved quietly, watched everything, and waited for my moment.

And when the moment came—I hit.

It didn't matter how many people said no. It didn't matter how many pitches flopped or launches went nowhere. Because each miss taught me something, and each miss made the next move sharper.

That's what most entrepreneurs don't understand. You don't need to win every month. You don't need to be perfect every launch. You just need to keep showing up, adapting, and staying in the hunt.

When people don't believe in you, good—that means they won't see you coming. That means you get to build in silence —no noise, no distractions. Just you, your claws, and the next move.

Here's what I know for sure: no one believed I'd make it. Not when I came to America. Not when I started my first business. Not when I said I'd host a red carpet gala or lead global book award ceremonies.

And it doesn't matter. Because tigers don't need a cheerleading squad—they just need the next hunt.

If you're in a season right now where no one sees your power —good. That means it's time to sharpen it. Use the doubt. Use the disrespect. Use the disbelief. Every successful person you admire was once underestimated. What made them different? They didn't wait to be believed in. They moved anyway.

Remember: you don't have to win every time. You just have to stay in the jungle long enough to land your strike.

So, ask yourself right now:

Are you stalking your goals—or just hoping they show up?

Are you strategizing—or waiting for someone to give you permission?

Are you in the hunt—or hiding behind perfection?
The jungle isn't fair; neither is business. But both respect the bold.

Claws out. Eyes forward. You're not here to play cute.

You're here to win.

Tigers don't ask for space—they take it. In the wild, they mark their territory with scent, scratch marks, and presence. They make it known: *This is mine.* And when another predator crosses the line, they don't negotiate. They defend immediately, decisively, and without apology. That's not aggression. That's clarity.

As entrepreneurs, we often spend too much time trying to be liked rather than being respected. We're afraid to claim a lane because we don't want to step on toes. We're afraid to be bold because someone might judge us. But here's the truth: if you don't own your space, someone else will walk in and take it from you—someone louder, messier, and less qualified.

When I first started my business, I didn't know anything about branding. I just knew I wanted to help people—authors, entrepreneurs, dreamers. But the industry was full. The noise was deafening. And nobody was saving a spot for someone like me.

So, I claimed it anyway.

I didn't have a famous last name. I didn't have fancy credentials. But I had clarity. I chose to plant my flag and say: *This is my lane. This is my voice. This is my space.* I showed up consistently. Authentically. And over time, people started to listen—not because I shouted, but because I showed up like I belonged there. Because I *did*.

Like a tiger, I didn't need a pack behind me to make noise. I let my work speak. I let my wins speak. I let my presence speak.

You don't need to be the loudest voice in the room. You need to be the one who moves with certainty. People can feel it when you're solid in who you are. When your message is clear. When your energy says, *I didn't stumble in here. I belong here.*

That's what owning your territory looks like in business.

Becoming the tiger in business means:

- You walk into rooms with quiet power—not noise.
- You stop chasing validation—and start building empires.
- You protect your energy. You guard your focus. You stop explaining yourself to people who never built anything.

Mark your ground. Not with ego—but with excellence. Not with talk—but with traction. Let your results do the roaring.

Because in the jungle, space isn't given. It's taken. And once it's yours, you protect it—not with desperation, but with the quiet, undeniable force of someone who knows they've earned their place. That's how tigers survive. That's how leaders rise. And that's how your empire begins.

So, if you're tired of playing small…

If you're done waiting for your turn…

If you feel the fire inside but haven't let it roar…

It's time.

Become the tiger.

"Territory isn't gifted. It's claimed by those who stop asking."

- Nim Stant

CHAPTER 2

TERRITORY ISN'T GIVEN — IT'S TAKEN

MAKE THEM FEEL YOU: OWNING THE ROOM WITHOUT SAYING A WORD

The jungle doesn't hand out territory. You either claim it—or you get eaten alive. I learned this the hard way in a small room in California, on a day that nearly broke me. I had flown in from Arizona, landing after midnight, exhausted but hopeful. I had paid for the flight and hotel myself because I believed this was my chance to audition for a TEDx talk. I thought I knew what I was walking into. I didn't.

There were about fifteen of us in that room. I came in prepared for a two-minute audition, as per the instructions I had been given. However, I then watched the first speaker take the stage and speak for five minutes. The next person spoke for eight. Then another spoke for nearly fourteen minutes with slides, perfect posture, and practiced storytelling. I sat there thinking, "What is going on here?" It was clear—everyone in the room knew something I didn't.

I wanted to run. Seriously—I started planning my escape like it was a spy movie. I looked at the exit door and thought, *"Okay,*

I'll fake a stomachache, walk out slowly like I'm heading to the restroom... and just never come back." That was the plan. I was going to vanish like I was never even there. In my head, it made perfect sense. At that moment, disappearing felt easier than standing up and admitting I didn't know what was going on.

It sounds funny now, but trust me—it wasn't funny then. I was embarrassed. I felt completely out of place. Everyone else seemed so polished, so ready. And here I was, rehearsing my escape plan instead of my speech.

But I had come too far to run now. I had committed. I had sacrificed. So, when they called my name, I stood up, heart pounding, and walked slowly to the front. I looked at the committee and told them the truth: "I have no idea what just happened today. I only came prepared for a two-minute talk. But I'm here, and I'll give you what I've got."

And I did.

I started with movement—yoga and dance. I flowed into my message, embodying every word. I finished in a headstand. And then silence. A beat later, the room erupted in applause. Everyone stood. One of the committee members looked at me and said, "Welcome to TEDx."

That moment changed me.

Later, I found out the truth: this wasn't actually an audition. It was the *rehearsal* for speakers who had already been selected to deliver their TEDx talks. I wasn't supposed to be in the room as an official speaker—but someone on the committee had seen something in me and wanted to give me a chance. They were considering adding one more voice to the lineup. That's why I had been invited. That's why they let me speak.

I didn't know it at the time, but I had been given a sliver of opportunity—*and I took it.*

Not because I was the best prepared or because I nailed every line. But because I showed up. I stayed when I wanted to leave. I claimed my space, even when I felt like I didn't deserve it.

In business—and in life—no one hands you your space. No one gives you permission. You have to take it. You have to show up even when you feel unqualified. Because the truth is, tigers don't wait to be invited. They don't tiptoe into territory. They claim it. They mark it. And they defend it with everything they've got.

That's what it means to lead. That's what it takes to win.

Territory isn't given. It's taken.

Looking back, that TEDx stage wasn't just a speaking opportunity—it was a test of territory. I had stepped into a room where I didn't know the rules, wasn't as prepared as the others, and felt completely out of place. But I stayed. I stood my ground. I delivered my message. And I walked off that stage with more than just applause—I walked off with ownership. That's what it means to claim your space.

Tigers do this instinctively. In the wild, they mark their territory with scent, with power, with presence. They don't tiptoe. They don't wait to be invited. And when another animal crosses the line into what's theirs, they don't negotiate—they dominate. It's not about being aggressive for the sake of it. It's about certainty. Clarity. Power.

Entrepreneurship works the same way. You don't have to be the most experienced person in the room. You don't have to be the most polished. You don't even have to be the loudest. But you do have to show up with presence. You have to own your niche. Claim your message. Let people know—without even saying a word—that this is your space.

When you carry yourself with that kind of energy, people take notice. They may not know your whole story, but they feel your authority. That's the moment when the shift happens—when you stop competing and start owning.

The TEDx moment taught me something I'll never forget: territory isn't always given. Sometimes it's something you step into boldly, even when you feel unprepared, and make yours. So, if you're sitting on the sidelines, waiting for permission or perfect timing—stop. You don't have to be perfect. You just have to be undeniable.

Mark your territory—and defend it.

In the jungle, a tiger doesn't explain why it deserves the land— it marks it. Boldly. Visibly. Repeatedly. As entrepreneurs, we need to do the same. If you don't claim your space, someone else will.

Marking territory in business means making it *undeniably clear* who you are, what you do, and why you're the authority in your space. You do this not just with marketing—but with consistency, clarity, and confidence.

You mark your territory by:

- Owning a specific niche instead of trying to serve everyone.

- Building a signature method, framework, or result that no one else can replicate.

- Creating a brand so distinct—your colors, your message, your tone—that people recognize you instantly.

- Showing up again and again, even when it feels like no one is watching yet.

Look at people like Marie Kondo. Her name *is* decluttering. Mel Robbins? You hear "5 Second Rule" and you immediately think of her. They didn't wait for permission. They didn't water down their message. They planted their flag and said, "This is mine." You don't need to scream. But you do need to be so clear, so consistent, so *you*—that no one can question whether you belong.

Tigers don't roar for attention. They don't need to. Their very presence shifts the atmosphere. That's the kind of energy you want to bring into your business. Presence is about power without noise. It's the grounded, quiet confidence that comes from knowing who you are and what you bring to the table. It's walking into a room and not needing to prove anything, just *being* the authority.

You don't win in business by being louder. You win by being aligned.

When you know your message, your mission, and your market, you move differently. You're not reactive. You're intentional. And people feel that. They lean in. They respect it, even if they don't fully understand it.

This is why you must stop shrinking. Stop apologizing for taking up space. Start leading with energy that says, *"I belong here—even if I'm not the loudest voice in the room."*

That's tiger energy. That's presence. That's power.

I didn't start this journey with a seat at anyone's table. I built my own. When I founded the International Impact Book Awards, no one handed me credibility. There were no guarantees. No investors. No big publishing houses backing me. I was a single mom, building a global brand from scratch —armed with a vision, a mission, and a willingness to claim space that didn't yet exist.

I marked my territory by showing up consistently, serving authors with excellence, and creating an experience that couldn't be ignored. I didn't wait for the industry to validate me; I created something so powerful that the industry had to take notice. And now? We're hosting red carpet galas. We're interviewing on network television. We're helping authors become celebrity experts and build their legacy. But none of that happened because someone opened the door for me. It happened because I kicked the door open and said, *"This is mine."*

It's one thing to claim your territory. It's another thing to defend it. There was a time when someone tried to replicate my entire awards model. The language, the structure, even parts of my message—it was like watching someone copy and paste my vision. At first, I felt violated. But then I remembered something powerful: people can copy your tactics, but they can never duplicate your energy.

Instead of chasing them or calling them out, I doubled down on what made my brand powerful—service, experience, and presence. I focused on elevating everything: better production, deeper community, more impact. I made my space undeniable. Because when you lead from a place of authenticity, no one can compete. You don't defend your territory by reacting—you defend it by rising.

So, now I want to turn this back to you. What space are you not claiming right now because you think you're not ready? What message are you hiding because you're afraid of being too much? Where are you waiting for permission, when deep down, you already know it's yours?

You don't need someone to tell you it's your time. You don't need more credentials. You need courage. You need to remember who you are and why you started. You need to tap into the tiger energy within you and stop waiting.

You are the tiger. You were never meant to play small. You were built to claim territory.

Now claim your space—and defend it with everything you've got.

Everything we do as entrepreneurs comes down to one thing: **belief**.

You have to believe in what you're building. You have to believe in your mission, your message, and your vision—especially on the days when no one else does. Because here's the truth: there will be moments when people doubt you. They'll question your value, dismiss your work, or try to define you based on their limited perspective. And if you're not grounded in your own belief, their noise will start to sound like truth.

That's the danger.

It's already hard enough to build a business from nothing. You take a small idea, pour your heart into it, risk your time, money, and energy—and then you fight like hell to make it profitable. That journey is brutal at times. It will shake your confidence, test your limits, and make you question your worth.

But if you don't have that deep, unshakable belief in what you're doing—if you don't fully own your territory—then it becomes easy to lose your footing. And when belief wavers, businesses break. You start compromising. You start playing small. You let others define your space.

That's why belief isn't optional. It's everything. Belief is the foundation that allows you to mark your territory and defend it when it's tested. It's the fuel that keeps you moving when the jungle gets loud. And it's the fire that tells the world, *"This space is mine."*

You don't need to be the loudest. You don't need to have it all figured out. But you do need to believe.

Because territory isn't given—it's taken. And belief is what gives you the courage to take it.

I remember sitting across from a TV producer, pitching my idea for a show—sharing what I could do, the impact I believed we could create. But after I poured my heart out, she looked me in the eye and said, "You need to remember where you came from." And in a way, she wasn't wrong. I had no experience in television. I didn't grow up in journalism. I didn't even graduate in the U.S. And yes—sometimes my English still stumbles. From her perspective, I had no reason to be taken seriously. No credibility. No resume to back up my dream. The answer was a big, clear, "NO."

But I didn't give up.

Instead, I got to work. I spent the next few months crafting my art. Honing my knowledge. Building my skill set. I created new work, elevated everything I touched, and sent it back to her—not with words, but with results. I didn't chase her; I showed her. And when she saw it, her response was, "Who are you, lady?"

That moment changed everything. She believed me. She respected me—and she wanted to work with me. I didn't walk away when the answer was no. I didn't internalize her doubt. I stayed focused on the target—and I didn't let go until I won.

That's the tiger in me.

Tigers don't stop just because someone says no. They don't get discouraged when the odds aren't in their favor. They stalk their goals with quiet focus, and when the time is right, they strike.

That's the truth about belief—it's what keeps you going when nothing else is certain. It's already hard enough to build a business from scratch. You start with a small idea, sacrifice your time, money, and energy, and work tirelessly to make it profitable. That journey alone is hard. But without belief? It becomes nearly impossible.

Because when you don't believe in what you're building, it's easy to fall into doubt. You start shrinking. You start second-guessing. You let other people define your worth—and you start giving up pieces of your territory without even realizing it.

But when you believe, you become unshakable. You don't need the loudest voice. You don't need perfect credentials. You just need the courage to keep showing up—again and again—until they have no choice but to see you.

Because territory isn't given—it's taken. And belief is what gives you the claws to take it, and the strength to never let it go.

"You don't need to chase opportunity. You need to become so clear, it can't miss you."

- Nim Stant

CHAPTER 3

KILL THE NICE GIRL

WHY THE STRONGEST ENTREPRENEURS DON'T CHASE, THEY STRIKE

There's a version of you that was taught to be sweet. Polite. Easy to work with. To not interrupt. To not be intimidating. To shrink your voice so others feel comfortable. That version of you—the *nice girl*—can't survive the jungle of business.

She was raised to be liked. But in entrepreneurship, being liked won't get work done. Being effective will. Being strategic will. Being a killer—in your focus, in your energy, in your positioning—will.

This chapter isn't about becoming cold. It's about becoming clear. You're not here to chase every opportunity, beg for every sale, or wait to be noticed. Tigers don't chase. They stalk. They're silent. Calculated. Intentional. They own their space. You're not too aggressive. You're not too much. You've just been conditioned to believe that power is something you need permission for.

Let me be the one to tell you: you don't need permission. You need precision. To rise, you must kill the nice girl. The one who waits. The one who plays safe. The one who apologizes for wanting more. Because if you don't, she'll cost you everything—your momentum, your money, your mission. We live in a world where too many women are told to stay likable instead of becoming legendary. But likability won't build your empire. Pleasing people won't protect your profit. Playing nice won't get your work seen, your vision respected, or your offer paid for.

A tiger's body is built for domination. Its vision is focused. Its muscles are precise. Its silence is part of the hunt. It doesn't waste anything—not time, not effort, not attention. Everything serves one purpose: survival and success. As an entrepreneur, you have that same design. Your story, your background, your scars, your accent, your culture, your failures—they are part of your weapon. When used with clarity, they don't weaken your brand. They make you *lethal*.

But only if you stop hiding.

Entrepreneurship rewards those who stand out, not those who blend in. And if you're still trying to sound like everyone else, speak like everyone else, and play by the rules everyone else created—you're not hunting. You're hoping. And hope is not a business strategy. The moment you stop chasing is the moment you start leading. The moment you stop softening your message is the moment your voice gets heard. The moment you stop shrinking is the moment people start paying attention. That's when the shift happens—from nice to known, from overlooked to unforgettable.

So, if you feel like you've been playing nice, waiting your turn, asking for permission—it's time to wake up the part of you that remembers who you are. The part that's tired of holding back. The part that was never meant to be tamed. That's the Thai Tiger in you. She's not here to impress. She's here to *own*.

In business, too many people are roaring for attention before they've done the work. Flashy branding. Loud claims. Empty hype. But none of that creates long-term power. You don't need to shout. You don't need to prove your worth to everyone on the internet. You need proof. You need results.

A tiger's power doesn't come from noise—it comes from precision. Your power comes from the same place. It's in your discipline. Your strategy. Your ability to show up consistently when no one's clapping yet. It's in the work you put in behind the scenes. That's what builds momentum that no one can ignore. When you're doing the right work, the right people will feel it—even if you're quiet. When your brand is rooted in real value, it doesn't need to scream. Let your results speak for you. Let your wins make the noise. Let your clients talk about you. Let your reputation walk into rooms before you do.

This doesn't mean you hide. It means you move with intention. It means your brand is sharp, clean, clear—not desperate for attention, but commanding it effortlessly. That's what makes you powerful. The strongest entrepreneurs I know aren't the loudest. They're the ones too busy building to explain themselves. Too focused on serving to waste energy performing. They don't care about being viral. They care about being valuable.

Entrepreneurs waste too much energy explaining and trying to justify themselves, pitching every person they meet. They defend their dreams to people who were never meant to understand them. And let's be honest—most of us do it because we were taught to be nice. To be agreeable. To be "understood."

That's the nice girl at work.

She wants to be liked. She wants to be accepted. She wants everyone to feel okay with her ambition. So, she over-explains. Over-apologizes. Over-justifies. She gives long answers to short questions. She softens her truth. She shrinks her edge—all to make her boldness more palatable for the people who were never going to support her in the first place.

It's exhausting. And it's unnecessary.

You weren't made to explain your greatness to people who never earned a front-row seat to your journey. You weren't meant to sit in rooms trying to prove you belong. You do belong—because *you decided you do.*

The longer you entertain the need to explain, the more you delay your results. And in business, results matter more than reassurance. Results are the roar that speaks when you stay silent. Results are what the tiger leaves behind—proof that she doesn't need to be loud to be lethal.

The nice girl seeks validation. She needs everyone to feel good about her next move before she makes it. But the tiger? The tiger *moves anyway.*

This is your reminder: you don't need to explain why you want more. Why you're raising your prices. Why you left the old job. Why you launched the thing. Why you stopped returning messages to people who never respected your time.

You don't need to convince anyone. You need to *convert* your potential into action. Into results. Into momentum.

Kill the nice girl who feels guilty for wanting more. Kill the nice girl who's still waiting for permission. Kill the nice girl who keeps explaining instead of executing.

Because she's the one slowing you down.

The woman who's going to change her life, scale her business, and lead with power? She doesn't explain. She builds. She moves. She strikes.

She let the results speak. Let your work speak. Let your presence speak.

Because when you strike right, *you don't need a second chance.*

A few years ago, my business went straight to hell—and it wasn't because I didn't care or didn't work hard. It was because I was playing the nice girl. I was trying to please everyone. I kept asking for approval: "Do you think this is a good idea?" "Should I do it like this?" I let everyone have a seat at the table, not because they earned it, but because I didn't trust myself yet.

I wanted everyone to be part of my project, because deep down, I didn't believe I could carry it alone. I listened to all the wrong advice—how I should price my offers, how I should structure my sales, how I should market. And because I lacked confidence in my own voice, I let theirs speak louder. I wasted so much time in networking events that weren't really about business—they were more like high school book clubs. So much noise. So much gossip. So many "Oh, let me help you!" conversations that never led anywhere real. I thought I was building connections, but I was just draining my energy in the wrong rooms.

And I didn't know what I didn't know—until I was broke. Until I had nothing left but lessons.

I'm not angry about it now. But I won't lie—it was an expensive education. When you put yourself in the wrong room, you don't just lose time or money. You lose momentum. You lose clarity. You start doubting yourself in places you were born to lead. And all of it comes back to that one thing: trying to be liked, trying to be approved and trying to be the nice one.

Let me speak the truth: when you're still playing the nice girl —whether you're a woman or a man—they will take advantage of you. Not because they're evil. But because people can feel when you don't own your power. They will test your boundaries. They will project their fears onto your dream. And if you're not rock-solid in who you are and what you're building, you'll start shrinking just to keep their approval.

This isn't just about gender. It's about humanity. We all grow up with stories—stories that say we need to be accepted to be worthy, liked to be safe, approved to be successful. But those stories don't serve you here. Not in the jungle. Not in business.

If you want to build real impact, you have to stop needing approval—and start making bolder decisions. Stay in your lane. Claim your space. Build your vision, not their version of it.

Kill the nice girl who second-guesses herself. Kill the part of you that needs everyone's blessing. Kill the habit of asking people who've never built anything if your idea is good enough.

46

It's time to stop explaining. Stop shrinking. Stop waiting.

The only thing you need to do is move.

Bethenny Frankel is a perfect example of what happens when you stop asking for permission and start owning your vision— loudly, boldly, and without apology.

Before she became a business mogul, Bethenny was just another woman with a big dream and no connections. She started out broke, living in a tiny apartment, working odd jobs just to survive. She was told over and over again that she was too intense, too aggressive, too much. People tried to put her in a box. Smile more. Tone it down. Be more likable.

And for a while, she tried. She did the "play nice" routine. She tried to fit in, to make people comfortable with her ambition. But it never worked. Because deep down, she wasn't built for small talk or soft goals—she was built to lead.

When she joined *The Real Housewives of New York*, people underestimated her. They saw her as the underdog. She didn't come from wealth. She didn't have a husband writing her checks. But what she *did* have was an idea—and the grit to execute it.

That idea was *Skinnygirl*, a cocktail brand born from her own lifestyle, and completely unlike anything on the market. She didn't beg anyone to believe in it. She didn't run around trying to convince every "expert" that it was going to work. She built it. She marketed it with raw hustle. She kept showing up, even when people laughed at her ambition.

Eventually, she sold Skinnygirl for over $100 million. No co-founder. No fancy boardroom backing. Just her—unapologetically driven, focused, and lethal in her execution.

Bethenny has said it herself: "Don't try to be liked. Try to be respected."

That's tiger energy.

She didn't waste time trying to get everyone on her side. She didn't play the nice girl to make the business world comfortable. She brought power to the table—and she let the numbers do the talking. If Bethenny had played it safe, she'd still be asking people if Skinnygirl was a "good idea." She'd still be pitching her worth instead of owning it.

The lesson? You don't need everyone to like your idea. You don't need everyone to approve of your ambition. You just need to build it. Prove it. And strike when the time is right.

Stop playing nice. Stop trying to please everyone. Start being *respected.*

Because no one remembers the woman who played it safe. They remember the one who showed up, built it anyway, and sold it for eight figures.

You don't rise in the jungle by being agreeable. You rise by becoming the tiger.

The version of you that's going to build something unstoppable —the one who strikes with precision, who earns with power, who leads with presence—doesn't wait to be invited. She doesn't ask if it's okay to take up space. She marks her ground.

She watches quietly. And when the moment comes, she strikes without hesitation. If you're still trying to make everyone feel comfortable with your hunger, you're not hunting—you're hesitating. And hesitation is deadly in the wild. Playing small won't protect you. It won't elevate you. It only keeps you surrounded by people who benefit from your silence.

Tigers don't roar to be heard. They don't explain their strength. They don't need permission to move. You were never meant to be tame—you were born with instinct. With edge. With purpose. And every time you hold back, every time you ask for approval, you deny the world the fiercest version of you. So let her go—the nice girl. Bury the one who waited for permission. Release the one who softened her claws so others could sleep better at night. And let the tiger rise.

Let her power move in silence. Let her story speak through results. Let her leadership be felt—without apology, without permission, without noise.

In the jungle and in business, it's not the loudest that rules. It's the clearest. The calmest, the most dangerous when the moment calls for it.

You don't owe the world your politeness. You owe it your full power.

You don't become a tiger by reading about one. You become a tiger the moment you decide you're done shrinking—done apologizing, done asking for permission in a world that was never built to hand you power. This book isn't just about information—it is about awakening something that's already inside you.

Now, you've seen the jungle for what it really is. It's not fair. It's not safe. It doesn't wait for you to feel ready. You've learned that no one gives you territory—you take it. And once you take it, you protect it like your future depends on it. Because it does.

You've also faced the truth: playing nice makes you broke. Explaining yourself to people who don't understand your vision is a trap. Waiting for validation, chasing approval, watering yourself down so others feel more comfortable— that's not humility. That's self-sabotage in disguise.

And slowly, something's starting to shift. You've begun letting go of the version of you that plays small. The one who needed to be liked. The one who asked, "Is this okay?" That version can't lead. That version won't survive out here. And that version isn't who you came here to be.

What's replacing it is something much sharper.

You're learning to move differently—quietly, but with power. You're starting to see that your story, your background, your scars, your differences—those aren't weaknesses. Those are weapons. You're no longer waiting to be seen. You're building something that can't be ignored.

That's the making of a tiger—not someone who survives, but someone who leads. Someone who doesn't chase opportunities, but creates them. Someone who doesn't roar for attention— they let their presence speak. Someone who doesn't try to be everything to everyone—but is undeniable to the right people.

You've built the foundation. You've seen the truth. You've felt the shift.

Now comes the next phase.

It's time to lead like a tiger.

Let's move.

"The tiger doesn't explain why it hunts. It just hunts. Stop explaining. Start executing."

\- Nim Stant

CHAPTER 4

EYES ON THE TARGET

LOCK IN. MOVE FAST. FINISH STRONG.

Tigers don't chase everything that moves. They stalk one target —and they don't take their eyes off it until it's done.

If they burned energy running after every sound in the jungle, they'd starve. Simple as that.

Entrepreneurs need to learn this fast. I've seen too many people with big vision and big potential go nowhere because they can't focus. They start something… then start something else. They build halfway… then ditch it when a new idea shows up. They stay busy, but nothing gets done. No real results. Just noise. It's not because they're lazy; it's because they're undisciplined. They confuse movement with progress. And in business, that confusion costs you time, money, and momentum.

Here's the truth: if you're chasing five ideas, you're not hunting—you're wandering.

The most dangerous entrepreneurs I know? They pick one thing. One offer. One goal. One outcome. And they lock in, as if their life depends on it. No flinching. No hopping from one shiny thing to the next. Just consistent, clear action in one direction. Your creativity is a gift—but it becomes a liability if you don't control it. Too many good ideas won't make you successful. Finishing *one* great idea will. So, stop flirting with every opportunity that comes your way. Stop asking ten people if your idea is good. Stop jumping ship every time something gets hard or boring.

Pick your target. Lock in. And don't look away until you've killed it.

A few years ago, I had too many ideas and not enough discipline. One day, I wanted to build a course. The next, a membership. Then a podcast. A summit. A second book. I was excited, passionate—but I was scattered. I thought I was being productive. I wasn't. I was just moving without progress.

At the same time, I was listening to everyone. Asking people what they thought of my ideas. Letting their doubt creep in. Trying to do a little bit of everything to make everyone happy. You know what that gave me? A bunch of half-built bridges. Nothing finished. Nothing profitable. Just exhaustion.

One day, I realized: my business wasn't growing. It was stuck. And the reason was clear: I was chasing too much. I hadn't committed to one clear target. One path. One outcome. So, I killed the noise. I made a hard decision to go all in on one thing. One offer. One brand. One system. I cut the distractions. I stopped explaining. I stopped asking for opinions.

And everything changed.

Here's what I know now: When you chase five rabbits, you lose them all. Pick one. Hunt it. Finish it.

Don't let your creativity be your downfall. It's not about how many ideas you have—it's about how deeply you execute the one that matters.

So, choose your target. And don't flinch.

"A tiger doesn't chase five meals. It picks one—and makes it count. That's how you feed the empire."

YOUR HUNT EXERCISE: LOCK IN YOUR TARGET

Step 1: Name the one thing you know you've been avoiding, half-building, or overthinking.

Write it down. Say it out loud. Make it real.

Step 2: Ask yourself—if I only focused on this one thing for the next 90 days, what could it become? Don't just imagine it. Write the number. The result. The outcome.

Step 3: Eliminate the noise. What distractions need to go? What "side ideas" do you need to shelf for now? Whose opinion are you done asking?

Step 4: Make the tiger move and commit to one bold action today. Just one. Something that puts you in motion toward that target.

In business, distraction is the most expensive habit you can have.

Too many entrepreneurs are everywhere—trying to be on every platform, launching ten offers, mimicking five different experts at once. They're busy, but they're not building. They're moving, but not in one direction.

Laser focus is the difference between noise and power.

When you stay in your lane—when you commit to your specific mission, audience, offer, and strategy—your business becomes magnetic. Clients know what you're about. Your team knows what they're building. Your message hits harder. And every move compounds.

Your focus creates clarity for everyone watching you.

If your attention is scattered, your brand will be, too. If your goals change every week, your results won't show up. Staying in your lane doesn't mean thinking small. It means going deep, owning your expertise, and becoming known for something specific—and doing it better than anyone else.

Intention isn't just mindset fluff—it's your weapon. When your actions align with your intention, you move faster. Cleaner. Sharper. You stop second-guessing. You stop chasing comparison. You stop asking for permission. And most importantly—you stop bleeding energy. Because when your mind is locked in, your business becomes unstoppable.

THE BUSINESS THAT TOOK OFF WHEN I STOPPED TRYING TO BE EVERYTHING

A few years ago, I was doing *everything*. Coaching. Speaking. Building courses. Hosting retreats. Running events. Launching products. All good things—but all at once. Every week, I was jumping between new ideas, reworking my offers, adjusting my prices because someone told me I should. I kept reinventing the wheel... and I was exhausted. My brand was unclear. My team was confused. I was chasing sales, not building a business.

It wasn't until I sat down and asked myself one simple question that everything shifted: "What's the one thing I want to be known for?"

I killed the distractions. I simplified my offers. I stayed in my lane. And within months, my income doubled. My impact exploded. And my brand became magnetic.

I didn't need more ideas. I needed more focus.

ARE YOU HUNTING OR WANDERING?

Answer these questions honestly:

1. Do you know exactly what your core offer is right now? If someone asked, could you explain it in 1 sentence?

2. Are you spending 80% of your time on one goal—or juggling five? What gets the most of your energy?

3. Are you building systems around one business lane—or reacting to trends? Be real: Are you leading, or following?

4. What's one project you need to finish before starting anything else? Name it. Lock in.

Score Yourself:

- If you're not clear on three or more questions, you're wandering.

- If you're locked in on all four—you're hunting like a tiger.

When you try to juggle ten things at once, you're not being productive—you're constantly forcing your brain to switch back and forth. And every time you switch, your brain burns energy. You lose sharpness. You lose speed. You lose clarity.

It's called **attention residue**—and it's the silent killer of momentum.

Your brain performs best when it's locked in on **one mission**, one target, one task. That's when you access your deepest creativity, your sharpest problem-solving, and your most powerful ideas. That's what scientists call a **flow state**. And you don't get there by dabbling.

The tiger doesn't look left and right. It locks in. Every muscle, every breath, every ounce of focus moves in one direction—toward the kill.

That's what your brain is begging for.

You want to build something great? Stop dividing your energy across twenty ideas. Give your brain the respect it deserves. Focus on one mission—and go all in.

When you treat your focus like a weapon, your brain will reward you with speed, power, and clarity. You'll stop wasting time. You'll stop burning out. You'll finally start winning.

Your brain isn't built to handle five things at once. What it's actually doing is switching rapidly between tasks—and every time it switches, it burns energy, attention, and time. You think you're being productive, but your brain is drowning in distraction.

The **attention residue** is a term coined by Dr. Sophie Leroy. It means every time you jump to a new task before finishing the first one, a part of your brain stays stuck on what you didn't finish. That residue builds up and kills your performance.
In his book, *Deep Work*, Cal Newport puts it simply:

"To produce at your peak level, you need to work for extended periods with full concentration on a single task free from distraction."
And in *The ONE Thing*, Gary Keller drills it even harder:

"Success is about doing the right thing, not about doing everything right... You can do two things at once, but you can't focus effectively on two things at once."

When you give your brain a single mission, it rewards you with clarity, speed, and creativity. That's how you tap into the flow state—the zone where elite athletes, top performers, and, yes, entrepreneurial tigers live.

This is why tigers don't chase five meals. They stalk one. And they don't blink until it's theirs.

You want to win in business? Do less. But do it better. Protect your focus like your life depends on it—because your business does.

These books will train your brain like a tiger in the jungle:

- *Deep Work* **by Cal Newport**

    How to develop focus in a distracted world and produce high-impact results without burnout.

- *The ONE Thing* **by Gary Keller & Jay Papasan**

    A step-by-step method for finding your most important goal and staying locked in until it's done.

- *Essentialism* **by Greg McKeown**

    Learn to eliminate everything that doesn't matter so you can make massive progress on what does.

- *Atomic Habits* **by James Clear**

    Discover how small daily behaviors create massive momentum when aligned with one clear outcome.

One thing I want to remind you is that spreading yourself thin isn't always a mistake. In the early stages of entrepreneurship, it can actually be part of the process. You try different things. You say yes more often. You take on too much because you're learning what sticks, what fails, what you love, and what actually moves the needle. That's survival mode. That's experimentation.

And sometimes, you have to go through the chaos before you find your clarity. But here's the catch: if you stay in that mode too long, you'll burn out. You'll get stuck in a cycle of almost-started, almost-finished, and almost-successful.

The shift happens when you zoom out and ask—what's my real target? What am I building toward? When you finally decide on your target and lock in, that's when everything changes. You stop chasing approval. You stop grabbing at random opportunities. You start moving with precision.

So, yes, there's a season for spreading wide—but the season that builds empires is the one where you go deep. Focus doesn't mean doing less. It means doing what matters—with everything you've got. And whatever you start, finish it like a tiger. Eyes on. No flinch. Full strike.

"Clarity creates speed. Distraction kills."

\- Nim Stant

CHAPTER 5

THE SOLO HUNT

MOVING WITHOUT A PACK

Tigers don't move in packs. They hunt alone. Not because they have to—but because they can. That's what makes them deadly.

As a solopreneur, you'll have to learn how to do the same—build without backup, move without permission. And fight through seasons where there's no applause, no help, no map—just you, your instincts, and your belief that the hunt is worth it.

Most people will never know what it feels like to wake up broke but still bet on yourself. To sit in a room where no one sees your potential—and still choose to lead anyway. To keep building with no safety net, no team, no fallback plan—only fire. That's what the solo hunt is. It's when your pain becomes your fuel, when your hunger becomes your strategy, and when your mindset becomes the only team you've got—and it better be strong, because you're carrying everything on your own back.

In this chapter, we're going to talk about what it really takes to succeed when it's just you—no partners, no crew, no handouts. Just your grit, your vision, and your refusal to quit. This is for the ones who are still fighting in silence. Still showing up. Still chasing something no one else can see.

If that's you, you're not weak. You're not behind. You're the tiger—and this is your solo hunt.

I remember when I started building my business—there was no "team." There was no assistant, no strategist, no expert holding my hand. It was me, my laptop, and whatever I could figure out on YouTube at 2 AM I couldn't afford help. I couldn't afford failure either. So, I did what solo tigers do—I hunted anyway. I built my first website by watching tutorials with broken English. I wrote my first offers without a coach. I made my first sales without a funnel, without ads, without any strategy other than: show up, speak from the heart, and serve like hell.

I was broke, scared, and so uncertain. But I was never idle.

And I think that's the part people don't see. They see the brand now, the interviews, the events—but they don't see the silent years. The nights I cried in the car between meetings. The times I pretended everything was okay when I had $27 left in my account. The pressure of being a single mom, showing up strong, and still fighting for my dream in a country I didn't grow up in. I had to lead myself before anyone would follow me. I didn't wait for perfection. I didn't wait for permission. I built while bleeding. I kept going when everything said stop. And I learned one truth that I carry to this day:

When you don't have a team, your mindset has to become your team.

Your belief system becomes your co-founder. Your routines become your assistant. Your discipline becomes your marketing department. If you can master that, you'll be unstoppable when the team *does* come. The solo hunt isn't glamorous. But it's where you earn your edge.

SKILLS EVERY SOLO HUNTER MUST MASTER

When you're alone in the jungle, there's no one coming to save you. You either adapt—or you starve. And that's not drama. That's entrepreneurship.

If you're a solo operator right now, here's what you need to master—not someday, but *now*:

1. Self-Leadership

Tigers don't wait to be led. They don't form committees. They don't ask for a second opinion before they move. They trust themselves—and they act. That's the essence of self-leadership. In entrepreneurship, especially in your solo season, this isn't optional. It's survival. There will be no one checking in to make sure you followed through. No one will remind you to build your brand, post your message, pitch your offer, or show up with courage. That's your job.

Self-leadership means moving with discipline even when no one is watching. It means building your business like your life depends on it—because sometimes, it actually does. You can't wait for motivation, praise, or approval.

You can't lead based on how you feel that day. You lead because you decided to hunt, and quitting isn't an option. The truth is, most people hesitate. They doubt themselves. They get stuck in the loop of overthinking and second-guessing. But a tiger doesn't pause in the jungle—it strikes. Hesitation in the wild means death. In business, it means missed opportunities, lost revenue, and wasted time.

So, if you're building alone right now, understand this: your ability to lead yourself is the difference between staying stuck and breaking through. You don't need to be perfect—you just need to be decisive. Move with intention. Trust your instincts. And keep going until your results are so undeniable that others can't help but follow.

2. Emotional Regulation

Every day in business will test you. One moment, you land a big win. The next, you're staring at an email that makes your stomach drop. That's the reality of the hunt. You get hit with highs and lows so fast, it feels like whiplash. If you don't learn how to manage your emotions, they will manage you—and not in a good way. Most people don't fail because they don't have talent. They fail because they let fear, doubt, comparison, or rejection hijack their decision-making. They start driving their business with panic instead of power. But here's what tigers know: emotions don't lead. Instinct and intention do.

A tiger doesn't whine when prey escapes. It doesn't spiral when a storm hits. It adapts, recalibrates, and gets back to the hunt. That's what you need to do, too. Feel the emotion—but don't follow it. Breathe through the chaos. Pause before the reaction. And never let temporary feelings rewrite your long-term vision.

In entrepreneurship, you have to lead yourself through disappointment, pressure, and unexpected punches. And that requires emotional muscle. Because the truth is, your success is directly tied to your ability to stay calm while the world around you is shaking. Lead your emotions; don't follow them. That's the only way to stay dangerous.

3. Resourcefulness

Tigers don't wait for perfect conditions. They hunt with what they've got. No excuses. No complaints. That's resourcefulness —and it's one of the most underrated superpowers in entrepreneurship. Everyone thinks they need more money to succeed. A bigger budget. A better team. A nicer camera. But what you really need is more creativity. More scrappiness. More hustle.

In the jungle, survival goes to the one who adapts fastest—not the one with the most resources. The same goes in business. If you're hungry enough, you'll find a way. YouTube becomes your university. ChatGPT becomes your assistant. Canva becomes your design team. You learn. You figure things out. You take messy action until something works.

Resourcefulness means looking around and saying, "What do I already have—and how can I use it better?" It means turning what others see as limitations into leverage. It means building momentum with what's available instead of waiting for everything to be perfect. The world is full of tools—but they're useless if you don't think like a builder. You weren't meant to sit around waiting for help. You're meant to create. Improvise. Adapt. Win anyway. That's how tigers do it—and that's how you need to lead.

4. Selling with Heart

You are the face. The voice. The closer. And in the beginning, you're also the salesperson, whether you like it or not. If that makes you uncomfortable, good. Growth starts there. Tigers don't sit around hoping someone else will bring dinner—they hunt. As an entrepreneur, you must learn to sell with heart. That means standing behind your offer with such conviction that people can feel it. Not sleazy. Not pushy. But powerful.

When you truly believe in the transformation you provide, selling becomes service. You're not begging anyone. You're not chasing. You're leading. You're showing someone what's possible if they say yes. Most entrepreneurs stall because they're waiting for someone else to handle the sales, the pitch, the ask. But the truth is: no one can sell your vision like you can. No one can share your story with the same fire. No one else is going to care about your mission more than you do.

That's why you have to step up, speak out, and own your voice. Learn the skill. Get in the reps. Stop waiting to be "good" at it —just be *honest*, be *clear*, and be *bold*. People don't need to be convinced. They need to feel your certainty. When you sell with heart, you're not just making money. You're making an impact. You're opening doors. You're helping people solve real problems. And that's a skill worth mastering—because it feeds your vision and fuels your freedom.

5. Time Discipline

A tiger doesn't waste energy chasing shadows. Every move is calculated. Every step has purpose. That's how you need to treat your time. In business, time is your capital—and most people burn through it like it's unlimited. It's not. Confusion is expensive. Indecision is deadly. You don't have time to "figure it out later." You're either building or you're bleeding. Structure your day like a CEO, even if you're still answering emails in your car between errands.

No one is coming to manage your time for you. Discipline isn't just about waking up early—it's about eliminating the nonsense that keeps you busy but broke. Time is the only thing you can't earn back, so protect it. Move like a tiger: focused, efficient, precise. Because in the jungle of entrepreneurship, the one who controls their time... controls the hunt.

6. Confidence in Your Voice

Tigers don't roar to impress. They roar to declare. Territory. Presence. Power. And in business, your voice is your roar. If no one knows what you do or why you do it, it's not because you're not talented. It's because you're too quiet. You can't fake authority; you have to build it. And the only way to build it is to *use* your voice—consistently.

That means posting when you're unsure, speaking when your hands are shaking, and showing up even when no one's clapping yet. You don't need to be perfect. You just need to be *clear.* Clear about who you are, what you stand for, and what you're here to do. Authority isn't about titles. It's about repetition. Tigers don't strike once—they keep showing up. Again. And again. So, speak. Post. Share. Teach. Lead. Let the world hear your roar—until they know exactly who you are and why they should follow. Silence won't make you safe. It'll make you invisible. And invisible tigers don't survive.

These are your claws. These are your teeth. These are your instincts sharpened by repetition. If you master these six things, you won't just survive the solo hunt—you'll become unstoppable. When you can't afford help, your mindset becomes your team—and your jungle survival kit. Tigers don't have assistants. No one's scheduling their hunt or cleaning up their mess. They rely on instinct, intelligence, and inner strength to survive. Same with you.

"Lead yourself first. The rest will follow."

In the early stages of business, when you're broke, building, and alone, your mind is your strategist, your motivator, your closer, your problem-solver. Your thoughts become your team meetings. Your discipline becomes your COO. Your belief system becomes your sales force. There's no one to tell you what to do—so you become the one. And that's not weakness. That's your edge. Because when you learn how to think like a tiger—lean, focused, alert—you don't crumble when things get hard. You don't freeze when the world goes quiet. You stalk forward anyway. That's the secret: you don't need to look like you're winning to be winning. You just need to *think* like a predator. Stay sharp. Stay strategic. Stay in the game—until you're no longer the one hunting for help... because you *are* the help.

That was ten years ago. I didn't have a plan or connections. I didn't even know how to run a business—I was just figuring it out one messy day at a time. I charged too little. I worked too much. I stayed up late Googling how to create proposals, how to send invoices, and how not to look like I had no idea what I was doing. I was running on pure belief. Not confidence—belief. There's a difference.

I remember signing up for a mastermind that cost $8,000. It felt impossible. I applied for a credit card and got approved for $3,000. That didn't cover it—but I didn't panic. I didn't overthink. I just knew I needed to learn. I believed there was something on the other side of that risk.

So, I hid behind the couch late at night when everyone in the house was asleep. Quiet. Anxious. Determined. I entered my card number one digit at a time, whispering to myself, "You can do this. You'll figure it out." And I did. I didn't have a team. I didn't have guarantees, but I had grit. And I had the willingness to move, even when nothing felt certain. That's what The Solo Hunt looks like. It's not glamorous. It's not loud. It's you, alone in the dark, betting on yourself when no one's watching—and not knowing exactly how it will work but doing it anyway.

Here's something most people don't talk about: you won't win every time. Not every offer will land. Not every launch will sell. Not every conversation will turn into a client. You'll pour your heart into things that don't move the needle. And that's not failure—it's reality. It's part of building something real. The early stages of business are filled with missed shots and silent rooms.

But just because something doesn't work the first time doesn't mean it wasn't worth trying. You're learning. You're building your instincts. You're getting sharper with every move. What matters is that you keep going. Not blindly—but with resilience. You regroup, refine, and go again. Success doesn't belong to the people who get it perfect. It belongs to the ones who stay in the game long enough to figure it out.

"A tiger doesn't waste energy chasing shadows. Every move is calculated."

\- Nim Stant

CHAPTER 6
BITE DOWN.
STRIKE FAST.

BUILD LIKE A MACHINE, MOVE LIKE A KILLER

Business is not a hobby. It's not a "maybe." It's a life-changing decision that either builds your future or breaks it. When I say *bite down*, I mean lock your jaws on your vision and don't let go. This isn't about dabbling or seeing if it "works out." This is about deciding—truly deciding—that you're all in. I've seen what happens when people treat business like a side project. They get side-project results: small money, small wins, small life. It's not because they're not capable. It's because they never committed. They tried to tiptoe into something that requires a full-body leap.

A real business will test you. It will pull every emotion out of you—fear, self-doubt, fatigue, imposter syndrome. And if you haven't decided to *bite down*, those emotions will win. They'll pull you out before the reward comes. The early stage of any business is rough. You're doing too much. Wearing every hat. Hustling with no clear roadmap. You'll question everything. You'll wonder if you're crazy.

And still—you must keep building. Brick by brick. Client by client. Day by day. Because here's what they don't tell you: building a business isn't just about money. It's about *who you become* in the process. It's about discipline. Ownership. Focus. It's about *earning* the identity of someone who can carry the weight of success.

If you're not ready to commit—if you're not ready to bleed for it—then maybe it's not your time yet. Because business will break you before it builds you. It will strip you down to who you really are. But if you can bite down and hold on through that storm, your life will never be the same.

That's how I built everything I have—not with luck, not with the perfect plan, but with absolute conviction. I was willing to be uncomfortable, willing to be misunderstood, willing to outwork everyone, and build even when it wasn't working yet.

I didn't wait to feel ready; I decided I was ready.

And here's the second part you must understand. The jungle rewards those who move. When the opportunity comes, don't freeze. Don't second-guess. Strike. I've lost count of how many ideas I've seen die because someone hesitated. They waited for the perfect time, the perfect partner, the perfect plan. Meanwhile, someone else with less talent and more guts launched first—and won. Momentum doesn't come from planning. It comes from *doing*. The more you move, the more you learn. The more you show up, the more visible you become. And visibility creates opportunity.

In business, momentum is your oxygen. Lose it—and you're gasping for relevance. Keep it—and you become unstoppable. People call me a workaholic. I used to take that personally. But now? I smile. Because they're not wrong. I *do* work harder. I *do* outlast people. That's my edge. I know I'm not the smartest, but I strike fast, and I don't let go.

Here's the mindset shift: you don't need to hustle forever. But you *do* need to hustle long enough to earn your freedom. So, bite down. Then strike fast. Build like a machine. Move like a killer. No gimmicks, no fluff—just discipline and momentum. That's how tigers hunt. That's how legacies are made.

I'm terrified of heights. The kind of fear that grips your chest, locks your breath, and makes your hands shake. But a few years ago, I made myself learn how to rock climb—not because I wanted to become a climber, but because I wanted to train my mind. I knew that if I was going to be a real entrepreneur, I had to master fear, not avoid it. Climbing a fifty-five-foot wall when every cell in my body screamed to stop was never about the wall—it was about control. It was about facing something I couldn't manipulate and still choosing to move forward.

That's business. You'll hit walls that make you question everything. The only way to rise is to keep climbing. And when you finally reach the top and let go—trusting the rope, trusting yourself—you realize the power isn't in the height. It's in the mindset that got you there.

Business is no different than that wall. Every pitch, every launch, every hire—it's a climb. And most people get stuck halfway up because they don't trust their grip. They overthink every move, freeze under pressure, and wait for certainty before acting. But just like with climbing, you don't need to see the whole wall—you only need to focus on your next hold.

In business, that's your next sale. Your next email. Your next hard conversation. You build momentum one step at a time.

And the truth is, the higher you climb, the scarier it gets. There's more risk. More responsibility. But that's when your mindset becomes everything. If you don't train it—if you don't strengthen your mental muscle daily—the weight of business will break you. But if you do the work, if you commit to the process and keep showing up when it's hard, you'll build the kind of resilience that nothing can shake. That's what separates entrepreneurs who last from those who tap out.

Business is not won with flashes of genius. It's won in boring consistency—sending that follow-up email, tightening your offer, refining your pitch, over and over again. Most people lose not because they lack talent, but because they can't stomach the repetition.

And when the opportunity hits—when the lead is warm, the door cracks open, or momentum builds—you don't hesitate. You strike. Fast. Tigers don't overthink. They don't sit and analyze. They move. That's how you stay alive in the jungle. And in business, momentum is survival. Every day you stall is a day you bleed opportunity.

You want to scale? Treat your business like your life depends on it. Build systems. Track metrics. Understand your numbers. Know your client. Bite down on one core offer, master the delivery, and keep your costs tight. You don't need more ideas. You need execution. You don't need more products. You need more buyers. This is the wild. And only the focused, committed, and consistent survive.

Too many entrepreneurs move like amateurs—random, scattered, emotional. They wait for motivation. They try ten things at once. They pivot every time they get bored or scared. That's not how you win. Machines don't hesitate. They run systems, processes, inputs and outputs. They get predictable results. If you want to build a real business—not a hobby, not a hustle—you need to think and build like a machine—tight offers, clean delivery, repeatable success. Every part of your business should serve a function, and every function should lead to profit, brand equity, or growth. If it doesn't? Cut it.

That's how you build.

But now, let's talk about *how you move*.

You don't have time to sit around. The jungle doesn't wait—and neither does opportunity. You need to move like a killer—silent, focused, strategic. No noise. No warning. Just results.

Your competition is out there talking about it. You're out here doing it.

Killers don't announce their moves. They strike when it counts. That means stop oversharing. Stop seeking validation. Build in the dark, move in silence, and then hit hard when the moment is right. Business rewards the ones who can build with discipline and strike with decisiveness. That's how you earn your territory. That's how you win.

Once you've bitten down—really committed to the path—you stop entertaining other options. That's when things start to change. You're not casually testing the waters anymore. You're in—fully. No backup plan, no exit strategy. Just grit, skill, and repetition. You're doing the reps when no one's watching.

You're building the thing, not talking about it. That's what creates something solid, something that lasts.

But here's the part most people miss: once you've built the foundation, you can't just sit there admiring it. **You have to strike.** That's how the tiger hunts—lock on, bite down, and when the opening shows up, it doesn't flinch. It moves.

Business works the same way. You build with discipline, but you scale with speed. You don't get to the top by waiting. You get there by moving fast when the moment hits. You know what you want. You've been working toward it. Now you stop pacing and *pounce*.

That's the game: Build like a machine, move like a killer.

If you pause when it's time to act, momentum dies. Confidence fades. And worse? Someone else strikes while you hesitate. So, once your claws are in, once your teeth are locked—don't let go. And don't wait. Bite down, then strike fast. That's how tigers win. And that's how empires are built.

Sometimes, your moment only comes once. That one opportunity you've been working so hard for—when it shows up, you better be ready to take it. No second-guessing. No waiting around to feel more confident. Because here's the truth: most people lose not because they didn't have a chance... but because they didn't *take it*. Success doesn't come to those who wait—it comes to those who *decide*—decide to win; decide to show up no matter what; decide that no matter how hard or how long it takes, they're not backing down.

I've seen too many people sabotage themselves by overthinking, hesitating, or waiting for someone to tell them it's okay to move. Stop that. This is your shot. And if you miss it, you might not get another one.

If you want to build a business that lasts, you need two things: a rock-solid foundation and relentless forward motion. Most people only focus on one. They build systems, but they don't sell. Or they sell like crazy—but have no infrastructure to support the growth. That's why businesses collapse. It's not that they don't have potential, it's that they don't know how to scale without breaking. '

Longevity comes from doing the same thing with discipline, over and over, until it works—then doubling down on what works. No shiny objects. No jumping ship. Just repeatable systems and consistent results.

But let's be real: *systems alone won't save you.* You also need momentum. Momentum is the invisible fuel of every successful entrepreneur. It's what makes everything easier once you're in motion—but brutal if you stop. You lose when you pause. When you hesitate. When you slow down and second-guess. The jungle rewards those who move—not the loudest, not the smartest, but the fastest. Every time you wait, someone else takes the shot. Momentum is created by decisions—*fast ones*. Execution—*daily*. Not waiting. Not wondering. Just moving.

So, stop planning your next pivot and start reinforcing what's already working. Stack wins. Build the machine. Get better, faster, tighter. And when the opportunity shows up—strike like hell.

People who don't know me well—and even some who do—love to label me. "You're a workaholic," they say. I used to hate that word. It made me feel misunderstood, like something was wrong with me for being dedicated, like I needed to apologize for having drive. I tried to tone it down. I tried to "balance" more. But here's what I realized: people will always criticize what they don't understand. They'll tell you to slow down, take a day off, go binge-watch something and "relax." They act like they have all the time in the world to give you advice—but none of the results you want.

So, I stopped listening. I stopped explaining. I stopped trying to fit into their version of life. I don't want to sit around on weekends. That stresses me out more than the work.

I made an agreement with myself: I may not take full days off, but I'll take a few hours every day to recharge. That's what works for me. That's how I keep momentum alive. Because losing momentum is a luxury I can't afford—not right now. And the moment I stopped apologizing for that, I fell even more in love with the process. This isn't a rulebook for you. I'm not telling you to copy me. I'm telling you to find your rhythm—and protect it. Your speed. Your structure. Your edge. Not everyone will get it.

And they don't have to.

"The loudest in the room is rarely the one in charge. Build in silence. Let your success make the noise."

\- Nim Stant

CHAPTER 7
PROWL QUIETLY.
MOVE PUBLICLY.

AVOIDING EGO & CHASING LONGEVITY

You've come this far. You've fought through fear. You've claimed your ground. You've built something real.

Now it's time to scale it.

This is the part where most people slow down. They get comfortable. They start overthinking. They lose momentum. But tigers don't stop after the first kill. They hunt again. And again. And again. That's how they survive—and that's how you lead. This part of the journey isn't about doing *more*. It's about doing it *smarter*. It's about building systems, leveraging time, leading a team, and making decisions that grow your vision even when you're not in the room.

It's not always sexy. It's not always exciting. But it's necessary.

Scaling a business isn't just a strategy. It's a mindset—a commitment, a decision to stop being the one who *does everything*—and start becoming the one who *leads everything*.

This is your next level. Not just working hard, but also building something that works *without you*.

This is **The Tiger Code.** Let's move.

Tigers don't run around announcing their hunt. They observe. They calculate. They *prepare*. And when it's time, they strike —clean and powerful. This is how you scale a business that lasts. If you're always on Instagram talking about your "next big thing," but you haven't even tested the offer, you're not building—you're performing. Some of the best moves you'll ever make in business happen in silence. You build when no one's clapping. You work when no one's watching. You master the offer, fix the holes, test it with real clients, and dial it in so it delivers every time. This is where real confidence comes from. Not hype, not likes—but systems that *actually* work.

You don't need a big announcement. You need a solid foundation. I've seen entrepreneurs fail because they launch too early—too loud, too proud—with no backend support. Real pros launch quietly and scale smart. They don't need to shout about it. They let results speak. Once it's working, then you go public. Then you go big. But the quiet launch? That's where you earn your stripes.

Here's the trap: ego wants applause. Legacy wants impact. If you're chasing likes, you'll burn out trying to keep up. But if you're chasing mastery, the spotlight will find you. Tigers don't roar for attention—they roar when it's time to lead. Build your business in a way that outlives trends. That's how you scale. Not by making noise—but by creating something that *matters*.

So, here's your reminder: you don't need the world to see you building. You need the world to see you winning. Let them wonder how you did it. Let them think it was overnight. You know the truth. You earned every inch of it—quietly, intentionally, like a tiger in the wild. Stay sharp. Stay focused. Build in the dark, so that when it's time to shine, your success is undeniable.

"The loudest in the jungle doesn't win—the one who strikes with precision does."

Let's be honest—ego is expensive. It makes you move loud when you should move smart. It pushes you to prove instead of build. It gets in the way of decisions, partnerships, growth, and sometimes... survival.

I've learned that, in business, the loudest one in the room usually isn't the strongest—it's the most insecure. Real power doesn't need to be announced. And when you chase ego, you chase short-term attention. But when you chase longevity, you build something that actually lasts.

Ego tells you to launch before you're ready so people notice you. Longevity tells you to sharpen your claws in silence so when you strike, no one can ignore you. Ego tells you to fake it 'til you make it; longevity tells you to master it 'til you can teach it.

The tiger doesn't roar to announce its presence—it waits, watches, prepares. Then when it moves, it's done with precision. That's the kind of discipline most entrepreneurs never develop because they're too busy trying to be seen instead of building something worth seeing. I've had to kill my ego a hundred times in this journey. I've launched things that flopped. I've built offers that didn't convert. And every time I wanted to blame someone or something, I had to face the truth: real leaders don't feed their ego—they feed their vision.

If you want to stay in the game long enough to win, you have to trade the spotlight for strategy. You have to care more about your mission than your image. Because when you build for longevity, your results become louder than your words ever could.

So, here's the code: Let your product speak. Let your clients advocate. Let your consistency become your billboard.

Don't just look successful—*be* unstoppable.

I've always believed that my greatest success isn't in how far I go—it's in how far my clients and students rise after working with me. When I see someone I mentored land a major media feature, speak on a big stage, or build a business bigger than mine, I don't feel threatened—I feel proud. That means I did my job right. That means I passed on power, not just knowledge. And that's the kind of legacy I want to build.

I don't believe in competition. I believe in *creation*. I believe in helping others carve out their own path, using their voice, and building their empire—not by tearing down someone else's, but by rising with integrity and purpose.

Ego can't get you very far in that kind of work. It'll make you insecure when someone shines. It'll keep you small while you're busy pretending to be big.

I remember reading *Relentless* by Tim Grover—the man who trained Michael Jordan and Kobe Bryant. He talked about a rare breed called the "Cleaner." The Cleaner doesn't just play the game. He changes it. He gets the job done—no matter how big—and then moves on to the next mission without needing applause. No post. No press release. No need to be told "good job"—because winning is in his DNA. Jordan and Kobe weren't loud. They were lethal. Focused. Disciplined. They weren't in it for the praise—they were in it for the result.

That mindset? That's what separates the good from the great. And it's precisely what will make or break you in business. So, stop trying to impress. Start trying to *impact*. Don't be the person who needs to tell the world what you're building every five minutes. Be the one who's so locked in, the results start screaming for you. Let them underestimate you. Let them ignore you. Then let your work make it impossible to look away.

The more I grow in business, the more I see a pattern: the real winners don't talk. They just show up and get it done. These are the ones like Michael Jordan and Kobe Bryant—people who don't need to tell the world how good they are. They just prove it—over and over again. That's exactly how tigers move. No roar. No noise. Just results. A tiger doesn't stop to ask for permission. It doesn't sit around waiting for applause. It sees the goal, locks in, and finishes the job. Then it moves on. Quiet. Confident. Unstoppable.

That's how I run my business. That's how I train my team. And that's what I want for you. You don't need to prove yourself with words. You prove it by showing up, doing the work, and getting results. No drama. No ego. Just action. Be the tiger. Be the Cleaner. Get it done—and move on to the next mission.

That's why I admire the mindset of a cleaner. They don't talk about what they're about to do—they just do it. Then they do it again. They don't stop to celebrate because they're already moving toward the next goal. That's how tigers are wired as well—silent, focused, lethal. And that's how you need to operate if you want longevity in business.

But ego? Ego will pull you out of that lane. Ego will have you posting your plans before they're real. Seeking validation from people who aren't even in the arena. The minute you start building for attention instead of impact, you've already lost. It breaks your focus. And in business, losing focus is expensive. I've watched people burn through time, money, and opportunities—not because they didn't have the skill, but because they couldn't tame their ego. They needed applause more than they needed results. Don't be that person. Tigers don't announce the hunt. They just eat.

"Just eat" means stop looking around for who's watching and start putting in the work that actually moves the needle. You don't need to announce your next move. Just make it. You don't need to explain your hunger. Just feed it. You don't need to look successful. Be successful. Let the results speak for you. Stay focused. Stay consistent. Stay hungry. The jungle doesn't reward noise. It rewards the ones who strike—and keep eating.

Tigers don't talk about how hungry they are. They don't make a scene. They don't ask the jungle for permission. They just hunt—and eat. That's the code. And in business, it's the same. Too many entrepreneurs are starving, not because they lack talent, but because they spend all their energy trying to be seen instead of doing the work that feeds them. They want validation. They want applause. They keep announcing every little move, changing their bio, updating their offer, tweaking their brand colors. But results don't come from noise. They come from focus. Execution. Discipline.

The real players are too busy building. They're making sales, delivering results, and creating something solid. They're not posting to prove—they're producing. They don't need attention. They want authority. That's the difference.

The real players in business know success isn't the finish line —it's just a checkpoint. But here's the trap: the moment you start winning, the ego shows up. It whispers things like, "You've made it," "Take a break," or "They should all notice you now." That's the danger zone. Because while you're busy celebrating too loud, you take your eyes off the next step—and lose your momentum. I'm not saying don't celebrate. Celebrate, but don't unpack your bags there. Don't let the celebration become your distraction.

I've seen entrepreneurs get a taste of success, and suddenly they stop doing what got them there in the first place. They start showing off instead of showing up. But the real ones? They stay grounded. They know there's more work to do, more lives to impact, more levels to rise. They smile, nod, and get back to building. That's the discipline. That's the difference. So, when the ego creeps in, remind yourself: the mission isn't over. Pay attention. Listen more. Speak less. Do more. Your legacy doesn't come from how loud you are. It comes from how long you last.

Kobe Bryant was the definition of a real one. A Cleaner. A tiger in human form. There's a story about him that still gives me chills. After winning a huge playoff game—while everyone else was celebrating in the locker room, laughing, taking pictures, riding the high—Kobe sat quietly, icing his knees, focused. A reporter asked him, "You don't look happy, Kobe. Aren't you excited you just won?"

His answer was simple: **"What's there to be happy about? Job's not finished."**

That's the mindset that builds empires.

Kobe wasn't distracted by the scoreboard. He didn't need applause to validate his effort. He was already thinking about the next game, the next move, the next level. That's how he stayed great. That's why he kept winning.

Entrepreneurs, take notes. While everyone else is busy clapping for themselves, you stay focused. While others slow down after one win, you lock in harder. The job isn't done. The scoreboard doesn't define you. Your discipline does. Your vision does. Your ability to tune out the noise and stay on the hunt—that's what separates the talkers from the titans.

Don't just play the game. Master it.

As entrepreneurs, we wear every damn hat. You're the boss, the assistant, the writer, the sales rep, the creative director, the janitor—and some days, even the therapist. It's a lot. And if you're not careful, it's easy to lose yourself in the noise. You start responding to everything, fixing everyone's problems, doing all the things—and suddenly, you forget what you're even building.

That's why I check in with myself all the time. I ask, *"Where am I going? Why am I doing this? Is this moving the needle— or just keeping me busy?"* Being busy doesn't mean you're building. It just means you're distracted. If you don't pull yourself back into alignment, nobody else will. The danger isn't losing money. The danger is losing your focus. And once you're scattered, you're no longer the tiger—you're just another animal running in circles.

So, pause. Get quiet. Get clear. And then get back to work. The jungle rewards those who stay locked in.

As I'm writing this chapter, I feel more tiger than ever. Not just because I'm telling stories or teaching strategy—but because I can feel myself stepping deeper into who I was always meant to be. This isn't just about building a business. This is about becoming. It's wild how much clarity hits when you stop chasing validation and start living from conviction.

I'm not here to impress anyone. I'm here to do the work I was born to do. Quietly. Powerfully. Relentlessly. The more I write, the more I remember—I didn't come this far to play small. I didn't walk through the fire, leave my comfort zone, and rebuild from scratch just to sit back and admire what I've done. There's more to build. More to serve. More to become.

This is the season of owning that. And I hope as you read this, you feel the shift inside of you, too. You don't need to prove anything. Just become it.

"Stop shrinking to fit into spaces you were born to own."

\- Nim Stant

CHAPTER 8

DON'T EAT WHAT YOU KILL

HOW TIGERS BUILD EMPIRES, NOT JUST MEALS

Tigers don't hunt just to survive—they hunt to dominate. And when they make a kill, they don't waste a single part of it. Every piece fuels the next move. Most entrepreneurs treat every win like it's the final destination. They land one client, get one media feature, make one sale—and they throw a celebration like they've made it. But that's not how real players win. Real tigers multiply what they kill. They use that one client to get ten more. They turn that one win into a story, a case study, a media pitch, a testimonial, a training system. The win isn't the end—it's leverage.

This chapter is a wake-up call. You can't afford to build a business on one-off kills. If you're constantly hunting just to eat, you'll always be starving. The moment you land something, your job is to stretch it, repurpose it, and systematize it. Don't just celebrate the kill—turn it into your next opportunity. Use it to expand your territory. Don't fall into the trap of killing once and feasting too long. That's survival mode. What you want is empire mode. And that only happens when you stop treating your wins like trophies—and start treating them like tools.

I didn't grow up in business. I didn't study branding or PR. I was a yoga teacher—barefoot, broke, and teaching classes for $19 an hour. I remember driving across town with barely enough gas in the car, praying someone would show up. That version of me wasn't thinking about seven figures. I was just trying to make rent. But even then, something in me refused to settle. I knew I had more in me. I had the fire—I just didn't know what to do with it yet.

The turning point didn't come from a miracle. It came from stacking small wins and multiplying every single one. When I hosted my first event, only five people showed up—but I used the photos, the video, the testimonials, the confidence it gave me, and I made it look like the most significant moment of my life. I pitched it to the media. I used it to raise my prices. I used it to create my next offer.

That's when I realized something powerful: you don't need a big break. You need to learn how to turn every step into a strategy. That's how I went from yoga teacher to building a seven-figure brand—by treating every moment like it mattered, because it did. I didn't just eat what I killed—I multiplied it until I became a name people couldn't ignore.

Looking back, that transformation didn't happen overnight. It came from paying attention to every step I took. From seeing each project, each client, each opportunity not just as a job, but as a seed. And if you're going to plant seeds, you had better have a plan to multiply the harvest. That's the shift most people never make. They chase the win, but they don't prepare for what to *do* with it. They work hard, pray hard, dream big—but they're still asking, *"What if it happens?"* instead of preparing for *when* it does. And that's where the real breakthrough lives.

In my world, every win is a weapon—if you know how to use it. When I got my first article published, I didn't just post it once and move on. I sent it to potential clients, I linked it in my email signature, I brought it up in sales calls. That one win opened doors to five more—because I knew how to multiply it.

This is the tiger mindset. Don't just eat what you kill—*use* it. Turn it into proof, into positioning, into power. If you land a podcast interview, flip it into content, into credibility, into connection. If someone says yes to your offer, ask them for a testimonial, a referral, a story you can share. Leverage is what separates hustlers from builders. Hustlers work for every dollar. Builders make every dollar work for them. Learn to squeeze every drop from every win—and then stack them like bricks until your brand becomes untouchable.

Reese Witherspoon didn't stop at being America's sweetheart. She didn't ride the wave of her Oscar win and disappeared into comfort. No—she used her acting success as fuel. While most people were still clapping for her performance in *Walk the Line*, she was already building her next empire.

She saw the gap in the market: strong, complicated female leads were missing from Hollywood scripts. So, instead of waiting for the next role to come her way, she created the roles. She launched *Hello Sunshine*—a media company built on telling stories that matter to women. She took her influence, her credibility, her *first big win*, and multiplied it into something far bigger than herself.

That's not luck. That's a tiger instinct. That's the mindset of a cleaner. She didn't just sit around celebrating. She built a system. She hired a team. She invested in the machine. And eventually, she sold that company for $900 million.

You think that happens because she waited around for an opportunity? No. She *multiplied the kill.* She saw the win, honored it—but didn't stop there. She asked, *"How can I turn this moment into a movement?"* This is what it looks like when you treat your success like a seed—not a trophy. You plant it. You water it. You build from it. And you turn one win into a legacy.

If you want to build a life that outlives the applause, learn from Reese. Make your next move while everyone's still clapping. Be the one who multiplies. Be the one who builds.

Tiger. Cleaner. Leader.

Don't eat what you kill. This means you don't burn through your wins like a starving animal with no plan. Tigers don't waste energy on chasing unless it's worth it—and when they take the shot, they use every part of the kill to survive, grow, and prepare for the next move.

In business, it's the same. You finally land the big client, make the big sale, get the media hit—and then what? Most people celebrate, spend it all, and take their foot off the gas. That's why they stay small. That's why their success dies in their hands.

Real entrepreneurs don't just enjoy the win. They reinvest it. They multiply it. They build a system, a brand, a machine that feeds more opportunity. You don't kill for survival. You kill to scale. So, when you win—pause, plan, and plant that win back into your business like it's your next investor. That's how you grow. That's how you dominate—not by chewing through your wins, but by multiplying them.

Here are **five clear, actionable steps** you can take to apply the *Don't Eat What You Kill* principle in your life and business.

Step 1: Pause Before You Celebrate

Win a client? Land a media feature? Sell your first $10K package? Don't just throw a party—pause. Ask yourself: *How can this win work for me again?* Celebration is great. But only after you've turned the result into a repeatable system.

Step 2: Reinvest the Win

Before you spend it, split it. Use a portion of every win to build something that outlives the moment. Invest in:

- Your systems
- Your team
- Your brand
- Your visibility (media, PR, ads)

Step 3: Document the Process

What worked? What didn't? Reverse-engineer the win. Record the strategy, the pitch, the messaging, the platform. Turn it into a process that you and your team can repeat over and over. No guessing. No starting from scratch.

Step 4: Stack the Leverage

Use your win as a door-opener:

- Got a testimonial? Use it in ads.

- Landed press? Put it in your bio.

- Got results? Turn it into a case study.

Every win should lead to three more. Minimum.

Step 5: Stay Hungry, Not Desperate

Tigers eat, then move. They don't cling to one kill. Neither should you. Don't let your last win become your last meal. Use it to hunt smarter. Hunt bigger. Stay focused. Stay moving. Stay hungry for what's next.

When I started, I did it all. The hunter. The closer. The cleaner. And I thought the goal was just to land the next client. But real power came when I realized every win needed to be reinvested. That's how you stop surviving and start scaling.

Systems are how you multiply your time—and in today's world, that means using tech like a weapon. A tiger doesn't chase every meal. It watches. It calculates. It conserves energy for the right moment. That's what your systems should do for you: work while you sleep, think while you build, and strike when it's time to scale.

Here's the truth: if you're still doing everything manually, you're not building a business—you're babysitting a job. Automation is your first employee. Use tools like Zapier, Make (Integromat), or ClickUp Automations to connect your platforms so tasks flow without you. Build backend systems that send onboarding emails, issue invoices, tag customers, or even assign tasks to your team—without lifting a finger.

AI is your second brain. Use ChatGPT to draft copy, brainstorm ideas, write proposals, answer FAQs, and even build out systems. Use Descript to edit video content in minutes, or Otter.ai to transcribe your meetings instantly. Use Manychat to build bots that handle hundreds of customer questions while you focus on closing your next deal.

CRM tools like GoHighLevel, HubSpot, or Pipedrive let you track every lead, every conversation, every close—without forgetting follow-ups. No more sticky notes. No more mental clutter. Even your calendar should be automated. Use Calendly or TidyCal to book appointments and send reminders. Use Notion or Airtable to create dashboards that show you exactly what's happening across the jungle of your business.

When you build smart systems, you're not just scaling faster. You're creating *predictable power*—a machine that runs whether you're in the room or on a plane to your next opportunity. So, ask yourself: where are you wasting time? What can be done once and systemized forever? What can be taught to a machine so you can focus on the kill?

That's how tigers scale.

Team is how you multiply your energy. You don't scale alone. At some point, it's not about how hard *you* work—it's about how strong your *pack* is. But let me be clear: you don't need helpers. You need killers. People who own their lane, move fast, and protect your vision like it's theirs. People who don't wait to be told what to do—they show up hungry, ready to hunt.

I don't hire for comfort. I hire for character. For fire. For loyalty. I'd rather build a team of gritty, hungry underdogs than a room full of polished resumes with no heart. Because in the jungle, the fanciest degrees don't save you. Instinct does. Commitment does. The will to finish does.

Building a strong team doesn't mean acting like a boss. It means becoming a real leader—the kind who sets the standard by living it. Your team won't rise above your discipline. They won't care more than you do. So, if you want lions beside you, stop leading like a house cat.

You build culture by example. Culture isn't about perks. It's how you talk, how you show up, how you push when it's hard. It's how you handle the wins and how you handle the losses. It's how your team feels when they fail—do they hide, or do they grow? That's culture. That's leadership. I tell my team all the time: this mission isn't easy. But it's worth it. And if you're in, you're family. That means we fight, we build, and we win together. Want to scale? Hire people who move fast and stay loyal. Train them. Lead them. Then get out of their way—because a powerful team turns your vision into momentum. And in business, momentum is what feeds the tiger.

Media is how the tiger roars. You can be the best at what you do—but if no one hears you, no one pays you. In today's jungle, attention is currency. And media is how you print it.

Too many entrepreneurs are out here building quietly, hoping word-of-mouth will carry them. But let's be real: silence doesn't scale. Visibility isn't vanity—it's strategy. It's not about being famous. It's about being known for something that matters. Your message. Your brand. Your results.

When I started, I didn't have media teams or press releases. I had an iPhone and a message. I showed up. I spoke with fire. I told stories that mattered. That's how I got interviews. That's how I built brand equity—one post, one video, one stage at a time. Now I run a media company that makes authors into celebrities. But it all started with me hitting record.

Don't wait for the "right time" to get visible. The jungle doesn't reward the quiet ones. The tiger doesn't ask for permission to roar. You don't need to go viral—you just need to show up consistently, boldly, and with clarity.

Invest in media like your life depends on it—because your business does. Podcasts, reels, interviews, press features, email lists, Facebook ads, Messenger bots—all of it is your jungle drum. Hit it hard. Hit it often. Let the world know who you are and what you stand for.

And here's the kicker—**media multiplies what you've already built.** You don't just "eat what you kill." You turn every piece of content into leverage. Into leads. Into long-term brand power. Media isn't optional. It's mandatory. You're not just building a business. You're building a legacy.

If you're still doing everything yourself, you're not building a business—you're buying yourself a cage. Hustling for every dollar, chasing every client, and delivering everything with your own two hands isn't noble. It's exhausting. And it's the fastest way to hit a ceiling. Real growth happens when you stop thinking like a freelancer and start thinking like a CEO. That means putting systems in place, building automated sales funnels, investing in media that keeps your name in front of the right people, and hiring a team that thinks like owners—not order-takers.

You don't build an empire by being the hardest worker in the room. You build it by designing a business that works even when you don't. The goal isn't more clients—it's more leverage. More repeatable income. More freedom. Your job is to step back, see the whole chessboard, and start playing to win long-term. That means stop celebrating every single sale like it's the finish line. The real win is when your business can run, grow, and scale—without you having to kill for every dollar.

Build a machine, not a moment. That's how you win in business.

And never forget this—your time is the most expensive asset you own. Stop trading it for crumbs. Start building with strategy. Start leading with vision. You didn't come this far just to hustle harder. You came to create something bigger than you. So, stand up, build it right, and lead like the empire you're building depends on it—because it does.

"The jungle doesn't care about your feelings. It respects only your fight."

- Nim Stant

CHAPTER 9

THE TIGER WAY

WHY THE MOST DANGEROUS
ENTREPRENEURS DON'T CHASE

There's a reason tigers don't run in packs.

They don't chase noise. They don't follow hype. They move with discipline, study their surroundings, wait in silence—and when the moment is right, they strike. Fast. Final. Clean. No wasted energy. No emotional panic. Just cold, calculated dominance. That's the way I've built everything in my life. Not by trying to be everywhere or please everyone. Not by doing what looked "fun" or "popular." But by waking up early, working 100-hour weeks, saying no to distractions, and doing the same disciplined reps again and again—until I became dangerous.

But this discipline didn't start with business. It was born on a cold tile floor in Thailand, where I trained as a classical Thai and Indian dancer. While other kids were still asleep, I was already sweating. I went to bed at 9 PM, woke up at 4 AM, and walked in the dark to my dance teacher's house. No excuses. No weekends off. Footwork came first—an hour of repeating steps until my legs burned. Then hand movements. Then spins —one hundred non-stop turns without losing balance. Then full choreography for another hour. Before 7 AM, I had already put in three hours of work. That was my normal.

I carried that same energy into my business. To this day, I go to bed by 10 PM, wake up no later than 4:30 AM, and walk to the coffee shop near my house to start working—not scrolling, not planning. Working. Writing my book before the world wakes up. Then my content. Then my business. When I interviewed Brian Tracy, he told me something I'll never forget:

"I write every day like I eat and shower every day." That's it. No drama. No secret. Just discipline.

This is the Tiger Way. And in this chapter, I'm going to break down the four principles that fuel everything I've built: **Discipline over chaos. Reps over luck. Precision over emotion. Focus over frenzy.** The most dangerous entrepreneurs don't chase everything. **They choose. They commit. They conquer.**

Discipline is what separates dreamers from killers. Life is messy. Business is chaotic. Emotions will come for you—fear, doubt, insecurity, even boredom. And if you let those emotions run the show, your business will stay small. Every time I didn't feel like showing up, I reminded myself: **F*** the mood. Do the work. That's the rule. I don't negotiate with feelings. I don't wait for motivation. I move because the work needs to get done. That's it.

People ask me how I stay consistent. It's not talent. It's not inspiration. It's because I trained myself to stop caring how I feel in the moment and start trusting the bigger mission. When life gets hard, discipline is what holds the line. Discipline is how I survive the chaos and still execute with precision.

That's exactly what tigers do. They don't act out of panic. They don't sprint after every movement in the jungle. They study. They calculate. And when it's time to strike—they strike. Fast. Focused. Final. They kill with precision, not emotion. That's the level you need to operate at if you want to dominate in business.

You can cry. You can feel. But don't you dare let those feelings decide how you run your day. You can't grow a business if you need to be in the mood to move. You don't need hype. You don't need a pep talk. You need self-control. You need rhythm. You need reps. Discipline isn't punishment. It's power. It's what keeps you sharp when everything around you is falling apart.

This is the Tiger Way. You don't wait for peace. You move through the chaos with precision.

DISCIPLINE OVER CHAOS

Most entrepreneurs don't fail because they lack intelligence. They fail because they spend too much time scrolling. Looking for motivation. Watching reels. Hoping that one more Instagram video will finally make them feel strong enough to start the day. I know, because I used to be that person, lying in bed, phone in my hand, trying to find a quote to pull me out of my own mess.

Some days, I needed motivational music just to brush my teeth. Some days I didn't move at all—I let the emotions win. I cried. I shut down. I disappeared. And I thought that was normal. But it's not. That's not strength. That's survival on a low battery. I'm not telling you to ignore your feelings. I'm telling you— **feel it fully, shake it off fast, and get back in your lane.** Lock your eyes on the target. Remind yourself who you are. And move like you've already won.

Discipline is not something you find. It's something you decide —every single day. People keep waiting for the moment they "become" disciplined, like it's going to magically show up one day when life gets easier. It won't. Discipline is built in the dark, when no one is clapping for you, when your body is tired and your mind is making excuses. I didn't wake up one day as a disciplined woman—I became her. I built her. Through daily choices. Through boring repetition. Through saying no when saying yes would have been easier. It's not always exciting. It's not supposed to be. But I'd rather be bored and successful than distracted and broke.

What most people don't understand is that discipline isn't restriction—it's freedom. When you create structure, you buy back your time, your mind, your power. My calendar is tight because my vision is big. I don't "go with the flow." I don't wait to see how I feel. I set my non-negotiables, and I move. Because without structure, life will run you. Clients will run you. Your emotions will run you. Discipline is how you stay the boss—not just of your business, but of your entire life.

And here's the truth: discipline is not about doing more. It's about doing what matters and cutting everything else. It's knowing what to say no to. The scrolling. The shiny opportunities. The distractions dressed as "networking." Every time I say no to something small, I'm saying yes to something bigger. And on the days I don't feel like showing up? That's when it matters most. Discipline isn't loud. It's not sexy. But it will build your empire while everyone else is still trying to feel motivated.

REPS OVER LUCK

People love to talk about luck. Right place, right time. Right connection. Right moment. But I don't believe in luck. I believe in repetition. I believe in showing up so many times, in so many ways, that something *has* to break open. It's not luck —it's math. The more you show up, the more doors you knock on, the more times you swing—something eventually gives. But most people never make it to that point because they give up after five tries. Ten tries. They do a few reps and expect a win. That's not how this works. Business doesn't reward dabblers. It rewards people who go all in.

When I was writing my book, I didn't wait for inspiration. I wrote every day. Same time, same place, same routine. Even when the words sucked. Even when I was tired. Even when no one was cheering me on. Because repetition creates momentum, and momentum is what builds confidence—not talk, not thinking, not planning. But Reps. Execution. Again and again. There's no magic behind greatness. Just routine. Just rhythm. Just reps.

Tigers don't chase every animal they see. They train. They track. And when it's time—they don't hesitate. That's the result of instinct built through repetition. Precision comes from practice. Power comes from doing the same thing over and over until it's impossible to get it wrong. In business, if you only show up when it's convenient, you'll never become dangerous. You want to win? Then stop hoping for a lucky break. Build the reps. Build the rhythm. Build the muscle so strong that even on your worst day, your system still moves.

I live what I teach. I hired a personal trainer to come to my office and train me one hour a day every day—no excuses, no skipping. I walk 10,000 steps every day. I eat pretty much the same meals over and over again—not because I'm boring, but because I can calculate the result I want. I repeat my routine so I can keep my results. I want to be healthy from the inside out. I want to live strong, work strong, and hopefully die healthy. That doesn't happen by luck. It happens by discipline. It happens by doing the same things over and over—especially when no one's watching. If you want real results in your life or business, stop waiting for luck, a break, or someone to pick you. **Do the boring work. Do the reps. That's what guarantees results.**

This is what most people will never understand. They're too busy chasing quick wins and getting frustrated when results don't come fast. But the ones who win—*really* win—don't rely on motivation or miracles. They rely on rhythm. Repetition. Relentless consistency. It's not sexy, but it works. Over time, the reps build confidence. The confidence builds results. And the results build your empire. This is not random. This is not luck. **This is The Tiger Way.** You don't wait to be chosen. You don't wish for an easier path. You train, you sharpen, and you show up—until what once felt impossible becomes automatic. That's how tigers are made.

PRECISION OVER EMOTION

Kobe Bryant didn't build a legacy on motivation. He built it on precision. While most players showed up to practice, Kobe showed up at 4:30 AM—every day. He wasn't driven by hype, praise, or emotion. He was driven by obsession. By discipline. By the pursuit of mastery. He made 800 jump shots a day, not because he felt like it, but because he *had a standard.* That's the difference. That's what the world calls the Mamba Mentality. I call it The Tiger Way. Emotion might give you a spark, but precision is what builds empires. Kobe knew that. Tigers know that. And if you want to lead in business, you'd better learn it, too. You can't make decisions from a place of panic, frustration, or fear. You've got to train your instincts, lock in on what matters, and strike only when it counts.

As entrepreneurs, we don't have the luxury of reacting to everything. If you let your emotions run your business, you'll burn out fast. You'll make decisions from fear, say yes when you should've said no, and chase after things that drain you instead of build you. That's how businesses die—not from failure, but from emotional chaos at the wheel.

I've learned to separate what I feel from what I do. That doesn't mean I'm cold. It means I'm clear. I've had days where I felt overwhelmed, hurt, and unsure. But I still showed up. I still executed. I still moved. Because feelings don't pay invoices. Precision does. Clarity does. Cold decisions made from calm logic—*that's how you win.*

This is the Tiger Way. You don't pounce because you're angry. You don't sprint because you're scared. You strike because it's time. Because you've studied. You've tracked. And now you're ready to finish the job. Business is war. Those who lead with emotion die tired. Those who lead with precision—*they walk away with the kill.*

ONCE CHASE WHAT'S WORTH CATCHING

Tigers don't chase every rabbit in the jungle—and neither should you. They don't run just to prove they can. They study. They stalk. They move with purpose. Every step is calculated. Every chase is worth the energy. Because in the wild, wasting time and energy means you don't eat. In business, it means you don't grow.

I learned this lesson the hard way. When I first launched my *Go All In Fest*, I was brand new in the business world. I had big dreams, big goals—and no filter for who I let into my space. People came out of nowhere, offering to "help." They told me they could bring the crowd. They said I should raise my ticket price. They said I should let them speak on my stage because *they* were the reason people would show up. And I believed them. Without question. Without hesitation. I thought they were my answer.

But what they really did was take advantage of my hard work and my money. They didn't bring value—they brought drama. They overpromised, underdelivered, and disappeared when things got hard. I trusted too easily, said yes too fast, and paid the price. I almost filed for bankruptcy after that event. And I'll never forget how that felt.

Now? I protect my focus like a weapon. I stay in my lane. I don't chase energy that isn't aligned. Just because someone talks loudly doesn't mean they know what they're doing. And just because something sounds like an opportunity doesn't mean it's worth your attention. Not everything deserves your time. Not everyone deserves your access.

This is The Tiger Way: **Don't chase what won't feed your future.** Your time is your currency. Your energy is sacred. Your focus is everything. Pick your target. Ignore the noise. And move like a leader who knows exactly where they're going.

Discipline. Reps. Focus. Precision. That's how I built everything. Not from hype. Not from luck. And definitely not from emotion. You don't get far by being soft. You get far by getting clear by doing the hard things over and over— especially when no one's watching.

I've made mistakes. I've chased the wrong people. I've said yes when I should've walked away. I've let my emotions lead when I should've moved with strategy. And every time, it cost me. That's a lesson I don't forget.

Now? I move differently. I don't react—I decide. I don't chase —I choose. I don't ask—I execute. Because I'm not here to survive. I'm here to dominate. This path isn't for the distracted. It's for the ones who are locked in. Sharpened. Unapologetically focused.

So, remember this: **You don't have to do more. You just have to move like it matters.**

Protect your energy. Cut the noise. And when it's time to strike —don't miss.

This is The Tiger Way.

"Everyone wants your attention. Not everyone deserves access to your energy."

\- Nim Stant

CHAPTER 10

PROTECT THE FIRE

THE DISCIPLINE OF GUARDING YOUR VISIONS, ENERGY, & INNER CIRCLE

You can survive in the jungle with wounds. But you won't survive if you lose your fire.

That's what I learned the hard way—not from a book, not from a podcast, but from real scars.

Early in my entrepreneurial journey, I made a mistake I see too many leaders make—I let too many people into my fire.

I used to say yes to every networking event, every meeting, every coffee chat. I was hungry to learn, to grow, to find "the secret" to success. I met people who spoke confidently, gave me advice, and told me what to do next in my business. And I listened. I believed them. I acted on their words.

But I didn't realize I was slowly giving away my power.

The more advice I took, the more disconnected I became from my true vision. I was no longer building my dream—I was piecing together other people's dreams. And my business? It didn't grow. It crumbled. I failed as a businesswoman, as a mother, and as a leader to myself.

Why? Because I didn't protect the fire.

And then it got worse.

I brought someone into the business who I deeply trusted—someone I thought would help me scale, lead, and build. But the more I worked, the more the energy in the company started to shift. Toxicity crept in. Conflicts brewed. Gossip. Blame. Finger-pointing.

I tried everything to restore the culture. Meetings. Trainings. Second chances. But the fire was fading.

So, I did the hardest thing I've ever done in business: I fired the entire team. In one day.

No second-guessing. No fear. Just clarity. Because I knew one thing—my fire was worth more than keeping the peace.

The fire is your clarity. Your focus. Your alignment with why you started in the first place. And if you let the wrong people in... you don't just get burned. You burn out.

That moment was a rebirth. I had no team. No help. But I had something more important: full focus.

And from that fire, I rebuilt.

Slowly, I rehired. But this time, I chose people not just for skill —but for spirit. For alignment. For the kind of quiet strength that doesn't gossip behind closed doors, but defends the mission when no one's watching.

Was it easy? No. Was it worth it? Absolutely.

Entrepreneurship is a war zone of distractions. Everyone has an opinion. Everyone has a "better" way. But the most dangerous entrepreneurs—the tigers—know how to say no. They know how to stay locked in. They don't give their vision away for validation. They protect it with everything they have.

Here's what I learned:

- Not everyone deserves access to your fire.
- Your vision must be louder than other people's opinions.
- If something or someone drains your energy—it has to go.
- You don't build great empires by being liked. You build them by being clear.

I used to fear conflict. Now I fear disconnection from my mission.

That's the Tiger Way: Eyes locked on the target. Fire protected. Distractions eliminated.

And because I protected the fire, it's still burning—and it's burning brighter than ever.

HOW KILLERS PROTECT THE FIRE

1. Audit the Leak

You're not tired. You're just distracted.

Every week, ask yourself:

- Who's draining me?

- What's distracting me?

- What's producing nothing?

Cut 10%: People. Tasks. Meetings. Content. It doesn't matter —**if it's not feeding the fire, it's stealing it.**

Tigers don't chase everything. They conserve energy and strike only when it counts. Do the same.

2. Stop Taking Advice from Losers

This one's simple.

Don't take business advice from people who don't have the business you want. Don't take money advice from broke people. Don't take life advice from anyone you wouldn't trade places with.

Tigers don't ask sheep how to hunt.

If they don't live it, don't listen to it.

3. Cut Fast, Heal Faster

If someone is off—cut.

It doesn't matter how long they've been with you; it doesn't matter how nice they are. If the vibe's off, the energy drops, or the culture shifts... they go.

You don't wait to see if a virus heals itself. You cut it out and move on.

This is how you protect the fire.

4. Control Your Environment or Be Controlled

You either own your time—or someone else does.

Turn off notifications. Cancel useless meetings. Stop letting broke people schedule your day.

Tigers don't multitask. They stalk, they strike, they eat. One thing at a time. That's how you win.

Discipline isn't sexy. But it's what scales.

5. Only Move with Killers

You don't need more helpers. You need people who can hunt.

Hire for hunger, not polish.

Hire for loyalty, not convenience.

Hire the person who thinks like an owner—not the one who asks what time lunch is.

If they don't bleed for the mission, they're a cost—not an asset.

Surround yourself with killers. Not caretakers.

Every distraction is a withdrawal from your fire.

You don't lose focus all at once. You lose it one "Got a minute?" at a time. Every time you stop mid-flow to check a message, explain your vision to someone who doesn't get it, fix a problem that someone else should've handled, or entertain an unqualified opinion—you're not just losing time. You're leaking fire.

That fire is your mental bandwidth, your emotional stamina, your strategic edge. And you only get so much of it in a day. Once it's gone, your creativity dries up, your clarity fades, and your leadership falters. In the jungle of business, when you lose your edge, you become prey. Someone hungrier, sharper, and more focused takes the shot you missed.

Research shows that when your brain is interrupted—even by something small—it takes up to twenty-three minutes to refocus fully. So, when you say yes to a three-minute distraction, you're really saying no to thirty minutes of momentum. Stack that over the day, and you've just burned through your empire-building hours solving someone else's emergency or explaining yourself to someone who wasn't even listening.

Tigers don't chase squirrels. They don't get pulled off course by noise. They lock in. They conserve energy. They stalk with precision. Why? Because even the apex predator doesn't have energy to waste. Efficiency isn't a luxury—it's survival. Tigers don't fight battles that aren't worth bleeding for. So, why are you?

Saying yes to interruptions means saying no to execution. Solving other people's problems means ignoring your own vision. Overexplaining your value to the wrong people means underdelivering to the right ones. You can't burn for everyone. You can't pour into things that don't pour back. And you can't keep your fire alive if you're handing out matches all day.

Protect the fire because you are the fire. And everything you've worked for dies if you let the wrong person touch the flame.

Fire isn't hype. It's not motivation or some flashy morning routine. Fire is focus. And in the life of an entrepreneur, focus is everything.

No one's coming to check your work. There's no teacher handing out grades, no boss tracking your hours. It's just you— your vision, your choices, and how you manage your time. That means if you lose your focus, you lose your fire. And when the fire goes out, everything else starts to fall apart. Your clarity. Your energy. Your team. Your momentum. Your mission. Gone.

It happens slowly at first—a few distractions, a few people pleasing moments, a few things you say yes to that don't align. Then one day, you look up, and you're not even building your dream anymore. You're running in circles, solving everyone else's problems, working hard, and going nowhere.

That's why protecting your fire is non-negotiable—because fire fuels everything. Your strategy. Your creativity. Your discipline. Your ability to lead. Lose it—and what you built can collapse overnight.

In the jungle, the tiger doesn't let anything dim its focus. It doesn't chase every noise. It doesn't spread its energy thin. It locks in, conserves strength, and strikes when the time is right.

You've got to do the same.

Say no more often. Guard your calendar. Be ruthless with your time. Not because you're too good—but because the fire inside you is too important. It's the difference between building something legendary… and burning out in the shadows.

Protect the fire. That's how you survive the jungle. That's how you win.

That's the Tiger Way.

"You don't build great empires by being liked.
You build them by being clear."

- Nim Stant

CHAPTER 11

THERE'S BLOOD ON THE THRONE

EVERYONE WANTS THE CROWN. NO ONE WANTS THE SCARS.

Throughout my time in business, I've heard people say they want to make a million dollars, build passive income, or create something that works while they sleep. But almost no one talks about the hard days, the brutal nights, the heartbreak behind the scenes. Nobody mentions the crying you do in silence, the nights you lie awake wondering if you're crazy for even trying.

When I first stepped into entrepreneurship, I had nothing. No capital. No connections. No roadmap. It wasn't about building a dream—it was about survival. It was about figuring out how to pay rent and feed my children. My start wasn't glamorous. It was gritty, raw, and full of uncertainty. And that's exactly what lit the fire in me. That desperation didn't break me—it made me fierce. It made me unstoppable. Once you've faced that level of pressure, you stop fearing rejection, judgment, or failure. You become something else. Something forged in the fire. Something wild.

Looking back now, I understand why the path had to be hard. I wasn't being punished—I was being prepared. The scars I carry aren't signs of weakness. They're proof that I didn't quit. They're part of my armor now. People want the success story, but they don't want the sacrifice. They want the crown without the cuts. But here's the truth: there's blood on the throne. Behind every empire is pain no one talks about—missed birthdays, lost friendships, the silence of isolation, and the weight of decisions that no one else can carry for you. You don't have to die for the dream, but you will have to bleed—because that's the cost of rising. The higher you go, the more you'll have to let go. The deeper you want to build, the more of yourself you have to give.

Tigers don't lead by committee. They hunt alone. They don't whine. They don't wait. And when it's time to strike, they do it with power and precision—often bleeding in silence to protect their path. That's the tiger way. That's the way of anyone who dares to build something bigger than themselves.

If you want to wear the crown, you had better be willing to earn it in sweat, scars, and solitude. This journey isn't for the faint of heart. It's for the relentless. The disciplined. The obsessed. You either bleed in the building stage or suffer in regret later. There's no soft version of this, only the real version. And the real version always leaves a mark.

Most people want the throne until they realize it's built on bones—bones of failed friendships, missed moments, and the pieces of your old life you had to burn to build something better.

And here's the truth they don't put in the motivational posts:

You don't get the crown without bleeding.

But the tiger doesn't just bleed anywhere. The tiger chooses when, why, and how. Most entrepreneurs? They're leaking energy, time, and self-worth all over the jungle floor—and they don't even know it.

Let me show you the mistakes that'll make you bleed unnecessarily—and how to stop the loss before it becomes lethal.

Mistake #1: Thinking Success Should Feel Good

We've been lied to.

Society sells us a dream that success should feel good. That if you're "in alignment," everything flows. The money shows up. The right clients appear. It's all ease and attraction. Laptop on the beach. Passive income while you sleep. Hustle is out, balance is in.

But let me tell you the truth—because I lived it.

When I first started my business, nothing felt good. Nothing looked glamorous. I didn't have investors. I didn't even have enough for rent some months. There were days I didn't know how I'd buy groceries for my kids. People think I was building a dream, but I was just trying to survive. I didn't start with capital; I started with hunger. Not the poetic kind—the real kind.

And through it all, I kept hearing the same messaging from social media: *"If it's hard, maybe it's not meant for you. If it hurts, maybe you're out of alignment."*

That advice would've killed my dream if I listened to it.

Here's what the research says instead: studies from Harvard Business Review show that the most successful entrepreneurs are not the ones with the most passion, money, or charisma. They're the ones with the highest tolerance for stress, uncertainty, and pain. Not just for weeks. For years.

And neuroscience backs it up—growth doesn't feel good. When your brain is rewiring to adapt to new challenges, it produces discomfort, even fear. That's not failure. That's evidence of transformation.

But most people misinterpret the pain. They think, *If this is my purpose, why does it hurt so much? If I'm on the right path, why do I feel so lost?*

Because the jungle doesn't reward the comfortable—it crowns the relentless.

That's why tigers don't panic in the shadows. They don't need to feel good to stay locked in. They don't chase dopamine. They chase the kill. The result. The win.

Success doesn't feel like peace. It feels like crawling through fire without losing your focus.

You want the crown? You had better be willing to bleed for it.

Tigers don't chase comfort. They hunt because they're built for it. You don't win this game by feeling good. You win by getting good at surviving discomfort longer than your competitors can.

Mistake #2: Waiting for Support or Permission

No one's coming—not your spouse, not your best friend. Not your mentor. Not the market.

This is one of the hardest pills I had to swallow early on. I kept thinking someone would show up and say, "You've got what it takes." I wanted a sign. I wanted permission. I wanted support. I thought if I could just prove myself a little more, someone would come along and open the door for me.

But the truth is—there is no door. You have to build it… and then walk through it alone.

In the early days of my business, I kept waiting for someone to believe in me. I'd explain my vision to people, hoping they'd see what I saw. But all I got were polite nods, confusion, or worse—doubt. I remember standing in rooms where everyone looked more qualified, more connected, more American. And I thought, *"Who am I to think I can do this?"*

But that's the thing. If you're waiting for someone else to crown you—someone else will take the throne.

Psychology calls this *external locus of control*—the belief that your fate depends on outside forces: other people, timing, luck. But entrepreneurs who win operate from an *internal locus*. They don't wait for green lights. They move like the road is already theirs.

Tigers don't ask the jungle for permission. They don't wait for the pack to back them. They prowl in silence, make the kill, and prove the power later.

When you're building something that's never existed before—there won't be a blueprint. And there definitely won't be a cheering squad.

Most people die with their dreams still inside them. Not because they weren't good enough, but because they were still waiting for someone else to say, "*Go.*"

You want to win? Move without applause. Act without permission. Bet on yourself so hard that the world has no choice but to pay attention.

Tigers don't ask the jungle for permission to roar.

Mistake #3: Trying to Take Everyone with You

You love them. They were there for you once. You shared dreams, ramen noodles, inside jokes, maybe even trauma. And now that you're climbing, you're reaching back, trying to pull them up with you.

I get it. I did the same thing.

But here's the brutal truth: **not everyone is meant to go where you're going.**

And the longer you hold onto people who aren't built for the next level, the more you'll bleed on the way up.

This was one of the hardest lessons for me to learn—especially as a woman, a mom, and someone who came from nothing. I believed that loyalty meant carrying people with me. I believed I could inspire them to change, to grow, to run beside me. But I was dragging dead weight. I was slowing down for people who weren't even trying to keep up. I confused love with obligation. Loyalty with limitation.

And I paid for it. In time. In energy. In pain.

Tigers don't run in packs. They're solitary hunters for a reason. Elevation requires silence. Focus. Precision. You don't see a tiger explaining its vision to the jungle. It just moves.

There's a quote I'll never forget: "The path to greatness is lonely—not because people abandon you, but because you outgrow the version of you that needed them."

Some people are anchors dressed like friends. Some are mirrors of your past when you're trying to build your future.

If you're still waiting for them to get it, you're already behind.

When I finally let go—of the wrong hires, the draining relationships, the friends who just didn't clap—I found a new level of energy I didn't know I had. I didn't hate them. I just couldn't carry them anymore. My dream was heavy enough.

So, here's the truth: You will lose people. And it will hurt. But if your fire is real—if your dream is sacred—**you'll choose the mission over the memory.**

Let them stay where they are.

Let yourself rise.

Because in the jungle, not everyone survives the climb.

Mistake #4: Avoiding Sacrifice Instead of Managing It

Everyone wants success. Few are willing to pay what it costs.

We live in a culture that romanticizes balance—soft mornings, self-care routines, working four hours a day from a laptop on a beach. It sounds good. But it's a lie—at least in the beginning.

Real success starts with imbalance. Late nights. Early mornings. Missed birthdays. Skipped vacations. Doubt from people who say they love you—pain from the people who actually do.
If you try to build an empire without getting uncomfortable, you'll either build something small or break yourself pretending it's supposed to feel good.

When I first started, I didn't have the luxury of balance. I was a solo mom, building a business with no money, no safety net, and no one checking in to make sure I showed up. I wasn't chasing a dream—I was trying to survive. That kind of hunger doesn't ask for permission. It demands sacrifice.

And I'll never forget this moment: I was interviewing one of the most successful businesswomen in the U.S. I asked her what she thought about work-life balance. She didn't even blink. She said, *"Work-life balance is bulls**t. School trains people to be ordinary workers. Entrepreneurship forces you to become extraordinary—and that takes brutal lessons, long nights, and real pain. If you can't handle that, don't start."*

That hit me. Hard. Because it was true.

Sacrifice is not the problem—denying it is.

Tigers don't waste energy. They don't sprint unless the prey is worth it. That's how you need to treat your time, your energy, your fire. Every move must be intentional. Every sacrifice must be strategic.

You can't give 100% to everything, all at once. That's not balance. That's burnout.

But you can go all in for a season—then recalibrate.
You can sprint—then recover.

You can bleed—then heal.

The mistake isn't the sacrifice. It's pretending you can avoid it.

So, decide what you're willing to trade. Decide where you'll bleed. And make sure it's for something that builds you—not breaks you.

Because no one gets to the throne without scars. But if you bleed with purpose, every scar will tell the story of your rise.

Mistake #5: Building the Castle but Losing the Crown

Here's the trap: You build something big. It works. You get momentum. But somewhere along the way, you forget who you are inside of it.

You're running the business, managing the team, pleasing the clients... and suddenly, you're a full-time operator in a machine you created—but don't even recognize anymore.

I've been there. The brand was growing, the revenue was rising, but I was shrinking.

My time wasn't mine. My vision got diluted. I wasn't leading —I was reacting.

I built the castle. But I lost the crown.

And that's the mistake. Entrepreneurs get so obsessed with scaling that they forget what they're scaling *for*. They pour everything into the thing and leave nothing for themselves. And by the time they realize it, they're trapped in a business that no longer feels aligned.
Here's the fix:

- Build the machine, but make sure it serves *you*.

- Design a company that gives you freedom—not just more responsibility.

- Protect your voice, your power, your identity—*or someone else will use it for their gain.*

You didn't start this to become a servant to your own success. A tiger doesn't declaw itself to fit in the zoo. It hunts. It leads. It establishes a territory under its control.

So, don't build a business that buries you.

Build one that frees you.

And if it no longer fits—burn the damn map. Start over.

Just don't lose your fire trying to keep everyone else warm.

Success is expensive. The invoice comes in pain, time, and trade-offs.

If you're not willing to bleed for it, don't pretend you want it.

People chase the image of success but avoid the cost—late nights, missed moments, uncomfortable decisions. They want the crown but refuse the cuts.

The reality? You can't have it all. Not at the start. You have to go all in on the build, or you don't get to sit at the table later.

Entrepreneurship isn't balance. It's imbalance, intentionally applied.

Stop expecting it to feel good. Start expecting it to cost something.

This is the tax on greatness—pay it, or stop pretending you're serious.

Because the throne doesn't go to the smartest. It goes to the one who didn't quit when it hurt.

If you're building something real, something that matters, you're going to feel the weight of it. Some days, it'll hurt. Some nights, it'll feel like you're the only one carrying the load. That's part of the journey no one talks about. But you're not weak for struggling—you're strong for staying in it.

Success doesn't come from the perfect plan or the lucky break. It comes from the person who refuses to quit. Who shows up on the hard days. Who keeps going, even when it's messy, uncertain, and exhausting. The truth is: there's always a cost.

Growth costs you time. Leadership costs you comfort. Impact costs you your old life. But if you're willing to keep moving—even with the bruises, even with the doubt—you'll come out stronger, sharper, and more focused than ever.

You'll realize the pain didn't stop you. It built you. And when you finally look back, you won't just see what you built. You'll see who you became in the process. That's the real win.

"You don't need to be invited to the table. You build the damn table—and then decide who sits around it."

\- Nim Stant

CHAPTER 12

DISRUPT THE GAME, DON'T JUST PLAY IT

YOU WEREN'T MADE TO FIT IN. YOU WERE MADE TO BREAK THE MOLD.

When I was just an author, nobody knew my name. I wasn't on TV. I wasn't in magazines. I wasn't speaking on stages. I watched my friends hustle for scraps—pitching themselves over and over, hoping someone in media would finally say "yes." They spent hours crafting the perfect email, the perfect reel, the perfect angle—only to be ignored. I saw authors begging to be featured, to be interviewed, to be picked. And I asked myself: Why does success have to look like this? Why should I spend all this time trying to be chosen when I could choose myself? It felt like everyone was following the same exhausting formula, just trying to play a game they were never meant to win.

So, I stopped playing. I built my own table. I launched my own TV show. I created my own magazine. I designed my own stage—and then I stood on it. And the moment I did, everything shifted. The same people who once ignored me started pitching *me*. They wanted to be featured. They wanted to speak on my stage. They wanted access to what I built. And honestly? It felt good. Not because I needed the validation—but because I realized I'd finally stepped out of the line and into my own lane.

That's what it means to disrupt the game. You stop auditioning. You stop performing. You start producing. You start creating platforms that solve your own problems—and in doing so, you solve problems for others, too. That's exactly why I built the **International Impact Book Awards.** I was tired of seeing authors treated like second-class citizens in the creative world. Actors get red carpets. Musicians get Grammys. But authors? They get overlooked.

So, I built a global awards platform that celebrates authors with the same level of prestige and visibility that Hollywood gives its stars. I didn't wait for permission. I didn't ask for approval. I didn't pitch myself into burnout. I just created the product I couldn't find.

You weren't made to play small. You weren't made to follow rules that were never designed for people like you. You were made to create new standards. When the world doesn't give you a seat at the table, flip the table and build your own. That's the Tiger way. Move like you own the jungle—because if you build it right, you will.

Most entrepreneurs don't fail because they're untalented. They fail because they play by someone else's rules. They follow the "safe path." They mimic what the industry is already doing. They look left, look right, copy what they see—and then wonder why they're invisible.

Let me tell you something no one else will say: If you're trying to stand out, stop playing the game. Start rewriting it.

Disruption doesn't happen when you blend in. Disruption happens when you choose to become the category. When I created the International Impact Book Awards, I didn't follow the publishing industry's playbook. I didn't sit around waiting for a committee or validation from some literary gatekeeper. I saw authors—amazing ones—being ignored, underestimated, and overlooked.

So, I created the red carpet for them. Literally.

No one asked for it. No one thought it would work.

But that didn't matter—because real change never comes with permission slips.

I looked at the way awards were done—rigid, exclusive, outdated. So, I broke the model. I made it global. I made it glamorous. Then I added *media*, *PR*, *TV*, *a stage*, *a spotlight*, and *a mic*.

I didn't build an award. I built a movement. And in doing so, I gave authors something far more powerful than a trophy—I gave them a platform.

Then I did the same with publicity: I didn't wait to be featured.

I became the one doing the featuring.

The rules only serve those who wrote them. If you're not the author of the game, you're a piece on someone else's board. Tigers don't ask for permission to hunt.

They move with purpose, alone if they have to. Not to fit in— but to dominate. Entrepreneurs who change industries don't follow formulas. They build new frameworks. They start messy. They take heat. They become the example others cite later.

So, ask yourself: Are you building to fit in?

Or are you building to become the reference point?

TACTICAL TAKEAWAYS: HOW TO DISRUPT THE GAME

1. Challenge the Norms

The marketplace often rewards familiarity. Industry insiders stick to templates—authors hop on bestseller lists, pitch agents, wait for traditional media coverage. That's why "safe" ideas multiply and real innovation stays hidden in the shadows.

Then comes someone like **Reese Witherspoon**, who turned that model upside-down. Instead of waiting for publishers or TV networks to choose books, she launched *Reese's Book Club* —hand-picking titles before publication, spotlighting stories by and about women, and leveraging her own platform to turn books into cultural moments. **70% of the books were chosen pre-release**, rewriting how publishing and influence intersect.

She didn't ask, "Is this popular?" She asked, "What's broken?" She saw a world where female authors were overlooked and transformed it from the inside out. Authors suddenly had TV sponsorship, social media buzz, and career acceleration—all because she chose to zig where the industry zagged.

Here's the Tiger Move:

- Identify assumptions in your industry.

- Ask: "What used to work but now fails?"

- Subvert.

- Launch fast—even if imperfect.

You don't wait to be invited. You build the stage and host the show. That's how Reese forced the publishing world to restructure its power dynamics—by building her own table and inviting everyone else to it.

2. Design Experiences, Not Just Product

Too many entrepreneurs stop at the product. They ship a book. Deliver a service. Run an ad. But if you want to stand out— *really* stand out—you don't just create a product. You create a *moment*. A movement. A memory.

Think of **J.K. Rowling**. She didn't just write *Harry Potter*. She created Hogwarts: Owls, wands, four houses, and butterbeer. Readers didn't just read—they *entered*. Theme parks, midnight release parties, costumes, and community. That's not just publishing. That's world-building.

That's experience.

It's the same reason my book awards aren't just about paper certificates and logos. They're about red carpets, spotlights, professional media, transformation, and timeless legacy. When someone walks our stage, they don't *feel like* an author—they feel like a star.

That's what people pay for.

They don't remember the page count; they remember how they felt. The moment their kids watched them win. The media coverage. The photos that made them *look* like the expert they already were.

So, ask yourself:

- What's the moment your audience will never forget?
- What experience do they *brag about* when they go home?
- Are you delivering a product—or building a platform that changes how they see themselves?

Products sell once. Experiences build empires. Tigers don't hunt for scraps. They hunt for territory.

Design it. Own it. Deliver it like nobody else.

3. Build the Platform You Wish Existed

When I was just starting out, I didn't need another "tips and tricks" blog post. I didn't need another gatekeeper telling me to wait my turn. I needed a platform—something real. Something that saw me, backed me, and gave me credibility when no one else would.

But it didn't exist. So, I built it.

That's how the **International Impact Book Awards** were born. I didn't want the authors just to win a digital badge and call it a day. I wanted authors to feel like stars. I wanted red carpets, press coverage, media interviews, lights, cameras—the whole thing. I wanted the world to view authors with the same admiration as they do Grammy winners or movie producers. So, I created the platform I wish someone had built for me.

That's the play.

You don't have to wait for permission to be chosen. If the doors don't open, build a new building. You don't need to fix the old system—you just need to build a better one.

That's what Reese Witherspoon did with her production company. Hollywood didn't give her the roles she wanted—so she started producing the kind of stories she knew women were hungry for. Today, Hello Sunshine is a media empire.

That's disruption.

Start with the gap you experienced. Ask: "What would have changed everything for me five years ago?" Now build *that* for someone else.

That's not just how you grow a business. That's how you change an industry. Tigers don't wait to be fed. They hunt—and then they build dens where others will find shelter.

You don't need to be invited to the table. You build the damn table—and then decide who sits around it.

4. Get Loud Early

Perfection is a trap dressed up as preparation.

You don't need everything to be flawless before you launch. You need two things:
A solid plan—and an aggressive timeline. That's it. That's the formula.

Most people overthink the start. They tweak logos, edit bios, obsess over colors, and copy for months... and while they're fine-tuning, someone louder, bolder, and faster already owns the space they were "preparing" for.

Look at **Mel Robbins**. She didn't wait for a book deal, a media team, or a polished brand. She showed up online with raw, real energy. She posted her thoughts. She taught what she knew. She built trust by being consistent, not perfect. And because she didn't wait, she created a movement. Her "5 Second Rule" wasn't just a book—it became a brand, a business, a household principle.

Why? Because she got loud *before* she got permission.

She moved fast and made noise. She let the audience grow with her—watching her evolve in real time.

I did just that when I launched the **International Impact Book Awards**.

I didn't wait for credibility—I *declared it*. I created a platform that didn't exist.

There wasn't a Hollywood-style red carpet for authors. No one was treating authors like celebrities. So, I said, "Let's give authors the Oscars moment they've never had." And then I told the world—even before I had the team, the systems, or the budget. I went all in with a vision and a tight timeline.

We launched fast. We filmed. We shared. We posted behind-the-scenes videos, author testimonials, media clips—and suddenly, *everyone wanted in*. Why? Because people don't follow polish—they follow momentum. They follow movement. And I was moving faster than anyone else.

That's how you win. **Don't wait to be perfect.** Be *first*. Be *bold*. Get loud before you're "ready."

While others are in beta… you'll already be the brand. While others are still testing… you'll already have receipts.

Success favors the tiger who roars—not the one who waits in the shadows.

5. Create Your Own Metrics

The moment you let someone else define success for you, you've already lost. Define your own scoreboard—and play to win *your* way.

Most entrepreneurs fail—not because they're not smart, not capable, or not driven—but because they measure themselves against someone else's scoreboard.

They think success means hitting six figures in six months because some influencer said it.

They think they're behind because they don't have 100k followers.

They think they're not legit because they didn't get verified or win an award from some outdated institution that doesn't even see them.

That's a trap. A distraction. And a straight shot to burnout.

You don't owe the world someone else's version of success.

You owe it to yourself to define what winning looks like for you.

When I was starting out, success wasn't a TEDx stage or a million-dollar launch. Success was being able to pick my kids up from school. It was not crying at the gas station because I couldn't afford a full tank. It was covering the bills without going into panic mode. That was my scoreboard. And every time I hit those small wins, I celebrated like I'd won an Oscar —because for where I was, I had.

Later, my metrics changed. I wasn't chasing a follower count— I was chasing impact. I wasn't asking, *"How can I look successful?"* I was asking, *"How many authors can I help become visible this year?"* That's how I built the International Impact Book Awards. That was my scoreboard.

Here's the truth most people won't tell you:

Industry metrics are made to make you feel like you're always behind.

They move the goalposts. They glorify the highlight reel.
 And if you keep chasing them, you'll never feel good enough —even when you're doing better than 99% of people.

So, flip it.

Make your own metrics.

Start with:

- What *really* matters to you?

- What do you want your life to look like—not just your business?

- What does *enough* feel like?

Then build your goals around that.

Want to work four hours a day and spend the rest of the time with your family? Great—that's success.

Want to build a $5M brand in silence without going viral? Do it —that's success.

Want to make $100K a year doing what you love, living on your terms? That's not small. That's freedom.

The most dangerous thing you can do is win someone else's game—only to realize it's not what you wanted.

Build your business. But build it on your terms. Measure what *matters to you*. Track progress that *lights you up*. And don't apologize for doing it differently. You don't need to fit the mold. You need to *own your lane*—and run it like hell.

So, here's the truth:

You were never meant to play by their rules.

If the industry doesn't see you, build something so undeniable they can't ignore it. If the doors don't open, carve your own damn entrance. If the game was never designed for someone like you, flip the board and start your own. That's what I did. Not because I had all the answers—but because I refused to stay invisible.

Disruption isn't about making noise. It's about solving real problems—the ones no one else has the guts to touch. It's about building the thing you wish existed, even when no one gives you permission, approval, or applause.

You don't need another course. You don't need a pep talk or a strategy call. You already know enough. You've already lived enough. You've already seen what doesn't work. What you need is to move—loud, fast, and unapologetically.

Build the thing. Launch the offer. Host the event. Film the video. Write the email. Send the pitch.

Not next year. Not next month.

Now.

Most people spend their lives preparing. They tweak, plan, overthink, and wait for perfect timing. And while they wait, someone bolder—someone like you—is already out there making it happen. You're not built to blend in. You're built to be the one they point to when they say, "That's what's possible."

You're not chasing validation anymore. You're setting the standard.

You're not asking for a seat at their table. You're building one so bold, so magnetic, so original… they'll come knocking. And when they do?

Smile. Pull out the chair.

Because that's what *you* do.

You don't just disrupt the game.

You become the game.

"Grit is the currency of the jungle. Pay daily or get eaten alive."

\- Nim Stant

CHAPTER 13

MONEY IS THE MEGAPHONE

MONEY DOESN'T CHANGE WHO YOU ARE—IT JUST TURNS UP THE VOLUME

Let's get this straight—money was never the endgame. Impact was. But without money, your message gets stuck in your throat. You can have the biggest heart in the world, the deepest purpose, the boldest vision—but if you're broke, no one hears you.

People love to say, "It's not about the money." But the people who say that usually don't have to worry about it. When I started this journey, I wasn't trying to be rich—I was trying to survive. Trying to feed my kids. Trying to prove to myself that I wasn't crazy for believing I could build something out of nothing.

But as I grew, I realized something important: money is a tool. A weapon. A microphone. It's how you take your story global, how you fund the mission, and how you stop whispering and start roaring. I didn't build a multimillion-dollar business just to have nice things. I built it because I needed the power to move things, shift things, build stages, and give others a voice.

You want to change lives? Good. You'll need money for that.

You want to build schools, start programs, donate, sponsor, fund dreams, and fly your team to new opportunities? You'll need revenue. Not one-time wins—systems. Engines. Recurring income. Scalable offers. This isn't about greed—it's about reach. Because without money, even the most beautiful dream dies small.

Let me say this clearly: if you're scared of money, you'll never make enough to matter. If you avoid talking about it, pricing your worth, or building for scale, you'll always stay small—and the people who need your message will never hear it.

Money is the megaphone. It amplifies your voice, your values, and your vision.

That's why I stopped apologizing for making money. I stopped flinching when I launched high-ticket offers. I stopped shrinking my prices to "be nice." Because I realized that every dollar I earn with integrity is another opportunity to change lives on my terms.

You want to give back? Start charging more. You want to serve bigger? Sell better. You want to go global? Get serious about your numbers.

This isn't about chasing Lamborghinis. It's about building legacy.

Because guess what? Broke people can't fund movements. Broke people don't have leverage. Broke people don't get to shape culture, write the narrative, or decide what gets seen and heard. And if you don't have the power to push your mission forward, someone else will push theirs instead—and they might not have your values.

So, build unapologetically. Sell boldly. Earn proudly.

Because money in the hands of a tiger doesn't just buy stuff. It changes the world.

You don't have to love money—but you do have to respect its power.

Take **Sara Blakely**, founder of Spanx. She started with just $5,000 in savings, selling fax machines door-to-door while dreaming of no-show underwear. As the business blew up, she turned her newfound wealth into purposeful giving. Sara joined the Giving Pledge and committed to donating most of her fortune. Through the Sara Blakely Foundation, she's funded millions in scholarships, women's entrepreneurship programs, and leadership initiatives globally. She understood early that her cash flow could fund opportunities for women who started with zero, just like she did.

Or consider **MrBeast (Jimmy Donaldson)**. He began as a broke teenager making challenge videos on YouTube. But as his channel exploded, he deliberately flipped the script: his viral content became a vehicle for generosity. Through Beast Philanthropy, he directs 100% of ad revenue and merch profits into social projects—from food relief and clinic-funded surgeries to #TeamTrees and #TeamWater campaigns that raised tens of millions for environmental causes. He didn't just chase views—he used his twenties to build wealth so he could make wealth go further.

These stories mirror what your money is capable of when treated as a microphone, not a trophy.

Sara didn't just want luxury—she built a company so she could fund dreams that matched her struggle.

Jimmy didn't just handle fame—he built platforms so his influence could feed, heal, and resource hundreds of thousands. If you're uncomfortable talking about pricing, scaling, or profit —you're cutting your own throat. Because impact costs money. Platforms, scholarships, stage opportunities, movement-building... it all needs capital.

Money in the hands of a Tiger is not vanity. It is velocity. It funds your mission. It wakes the world to your message.

So, if you're serious about legacy, ask yourself: **What would I build if money weren't the barrier, but the amplifier?**

Let that question fuel your next strategy, offer, launch—and scale unapologetically.

In the wild, a tiger doesn't chase everything. It watches. Waits. Measures. And when it moves—it moves with **precision**. One kill. One strike. Maximum return. No wasted energy. No scattered attention.

That's how you need to treat your money.

You don't need to do what everyone else is doing. You don't need a hundred offers, ten side hustles, and a million distractions. You need a *clear target*—and a strategy that hits it hard.

Here's the truth: Poor entrepreneurs hustle for survival. Smart entrepreneurs **position** for power.

You don't get rich by working more hours. You get rich by creating leverage.

You don't grow a movement by being everywhere. You grow by being **undeniable** somewhere.

A tiger doesn't roar all day—it roars once, and the jungle listens.

So, build your income like a tiger strike:

- One powerful offer that solves a painful problem.
- One platform that gives you visibility and volume.
- One story that builds unshakable brand authority.

Then scale the *hell* out of it.

Money is how you mark your territory in business. Not with noise—but with undeniable value. That's why tigers don't beg for attention. They **command** it.

You don't need to be viral. You need to be **valuable**.

You don't need followers. You need **buyers**.

You don't need one hundred products. You need **one empire offer** that funds your freedom, fuels your impact, and lets you roar louder for others.

That's the Tiger Move.

Not hustle. Not hype.

Precision. Position. Power.

Build it. Own it. Strike when it counts.

A tiger doesn't just hunt for today. She hunts to feed her cubs. To protect her territory. To leave something behind that *lasts*. That's what your money should do—not just buy the car. Not just pay the bills. Not just post the lifestyle.

Real wealth builds legacy.

It creates freedom for your children. Opportunities for your community. Impact that echoes beyond your name. You weren't made to just make money — you were made to *move money* with intention.

You don't need a trust fund to think like a king. You need *vision*.

Start asking different questions:

- How can I use my profit to build a platform for others?
- How do I invest in people, not just portfolios?
- What story will my money tell after I'm gone?

Tigers don't die quietly. They leave a mark. A trail. A bloodline that dominates long after the hunt is over.

That's what your financial life should do.

Make your money louder than your words. Let it build schools. Fund missions. Start foundations. Pay your team well. Create jobs. Buy your parents peace. Give your children a different future.

That's power.

And it doesn't come from playing it safe. It comes from playing the long game.

So, stop thinking in quarters. Start thinking in *generations*. You're not just building a business. You're building a bloodline.

That's the Tiger Move.

Roar for the world now. But leave a trail that roars long after you're gone.

You've come this far for a reason. Not to stay stuck. Not to stay small—but to rise.

So, stop waiting for a sign—this is it. The world doesn't need another silent genius. It needs you, loud and unleashed. With your story. With your skills. With your scars.

Start with what you have. Start where you are. With the fire you've been sitting on for way too long.

You don't need permission. You don't need perfect timing. You don't need a bank loan, a big break, or a fancy plan.

You need one decision: **I'm done playing small.**

Because when you stop chasing comfort and start chasing *calling*, money moves. People show up. Doors open. And if they don't?

You kick them open.

This is your moment. Your jungle. Your empire to build.

IT'S YOUR TURN NOW

Reading this chapter isn't enough. Inspiration without execution is just noise.

You say you want freedom. You say you want to be heard. You say you want to make a difference.

Then prove it.

These next few prompts aren't just journaling exercises—they're your battle plan. They force clarity. They eliminate excuses. And they give your mission a dollar amount, a deadline, and a megaphone.

You don't need permission. You need a plan.
This is it.

Now fill in the blanks. Get clear. Get loud. And take the first step like your future depends on it—because it does.

Tiger Action Steps: Make Money Your Megaphone

1. My Message Is:

What's the core idea, belief, or mission you want the world to hear louder?

→ "I believe _____."

2. My Money Goal Is:

What specific financial target would amplify that message?

→ "I will generate $_____ by _____ (date)."

3. My Revenue Plan Is:

Where is the money going to come from?

  → "I will focus on these 1-2 high-leverage offers:
_____."

4. My Impact Plan Is:

When the money comes in, how will you use it to scale your voice and help more people?

→ "I will invest $_____ into _____."

5. My Tiger Move This Month:

What bold action will you take in the next 30 days to move this forward?

→ "I will _____

by _____."

ONE LAST THING BEFORE YOU MOVE ON

Don't skip this.

Don't say "I'll come back to it."

Don't just read the next chapter.

Tigers don't overthink. They strike.

This is your blueprint. Print it out. Post it on your wall. Commit to it like your life depends on it—because your impact does.

Now go make noise. Your megaphone is waiting.

Money isn't evil. It's just energy—neutral until it's directed. In the right hands, it's not just a tool—it's a weapon. A lever. A megaphone. In your hands, it becomes something far more powerful: it becomes **proof that purpose pays**.

Don't chase money to impress people. Don't collect dollars like trophies to prove you made it. That's empty. That's noise.

Money isn't the goal—it's the amplifier. When you earn with purpose, money becomes your **loudest statement**. It funds your mission. It scales your story. It builds the schools, feeds the teams, buys back your time, and fuels the impact you were put here to make.

Every dollar is a decision. A declaration. A vote for what matters to you.

So, no—you're not here to hustle for likes or beg for approval. You're here to **build something real**. Something that lasts. Something that multiplies. And that means using money with precision and power.

This is the Tiger Move: You hunt with intention—not desperation. You build offers that scale, systems that work while you sleep, and brand authority that magnetizes opportunity. You stack with strategy, not ego. And when your platform is strong and your voice is funded—**then you roar**. You speak, you lead, you expand—and the jungle responds. The market shifts. The clients come. The doors open.

This isn't about greed. It's about **grounded impact**. Money is just the volume knob on your voice. The bigger your vision, the more it needs fuel. So, fuel it. Unapologetically. Boldly. Powerfully.

Because when a Tiger roars with purpose—**the whole jungle listens**.

"You don't have to love money—but you do have to respect its power."

\- Nim Stant

CHAPTER 14

LIGHT THE FIRE, BURN THE MAP

YOU DON'T NEED A PATH. YOU ARE THE PATH.

Everyone wants a map. Everyone wants to know the five steps, the exact plan, the perfect strategy to make it work. But the ones who make history? They don't follow maps. They carry torches. They don't wait for paths. They blaze them.

When I started this journey, I had no map. No mentor. No permission. Just a vision and fire so strong I couldn't sleep. I didn't need someone to show me the way—I needed to trust that my hunger would carve it.

And it did.

This chapter isn't for the person who wants to play it safe. It's for the one who knows something wild is burning inside but hasn't given it full permission yet.

STOP LOOKING FOR THE BLUEPRINT

The truth is—there is no "right way." What worked for them won't always work for you. The business world is flooded with recycled strategies, tired templates, and copy-paste formulas. But here's the thing: no one has your story, your soul, your scars. So, why would you borrow their steps?

Your story isn't built in someone else's footsteps. It's forged in fire. In bold decisions. In the nights when no one believes but you. That's where leaders are made. Not in the classroom. Not in a coaching program, but in the moments you bet on yourself before the results existed.

THERE'S NO HACK FOR HUNGER

Everybody's searching for shortcuts. Hacks. Scripts. But there's no shortcut for obsession. No script for soul. No hack for hunger. The ones who make it are the ones who go all in— even when there's no guarantee.

You want to win? Set yourself on fire for the vision. People don't follow perfection—they follow power. Conviction. Consistency. Energy. That's what moves the world. Not tactics. Not tricks. *You.*

YOU ARE THE PERMISSION SLIP

Nobody is coming to say, "You're ready." That's your job. The faster you stop waiting for approval, the faster your life will change. Because the second you decide you're enough, the world starts catching up.

People ask, "What if I fail?" But they never ask, "What if I never try?" What if the plan you're waiting for never shows up? What if the mentor you're hoping will guide you... never knocks?

Would you still build it?

You have to burn the map. Burn the need to be validated. Burn the idea that you need someone else to tell you you're good enough.

Because you are the fire.

THE TIGER MOVE: LEAD WITH FIRE, NOT FORMULAS

Tigers don't wait for coordinates. They follow instinct. They move on gut. They stalk what's worth catching—and pounce without hesitation. That's the kind of leadership the jungle respects.

You want to be the one they remember? Stop walking the trail and start torching it. Create the movement. Make the noise. Shake the cage. People don't follow the most "qualified" leader —they follow the one who's on fire.

WHAT TO DO NEXT: STOP FOLLOWING THE MAP & START FOLLOWING THE FIRE

If you're ready to lead, you can't wait to be told what to do.

You have to *decide*.

Here's how to start leading with fire instead of formulas:

1. Burn the Plan. Write the Vision.

Forget the 67-step funnel. Forget the color-coded planner. Forget waiting for someone to hand you the blueprint.

You don't need a plan. You need a direction.

Most people waste years obsessing over how to get there, but never ask *why* they're going in the first place. They chase productivity hacks. They map out marketing calendars. They study every strategy on YouTube. But deep down, they're stalling. They're terrified to move without a perfect path. So, they do what they've always done: wait.

But tigers don't wait. **They move.**

They trust their instincts. They trust their hunger. And they hunt with one thing in mind: the *outcome*.

If you want to build something real—something that actually shifts the jungle around you—you have to start with *vision*, not plans. Plans change. Vision doesn't.

So, let's cut the fluff. Start here. Write this down with gut-level honesty:

This is who I am:

The clearest, rawest version of your identity. Not your title. Not your job. Not your résumé. Who are you *when no one's watching*?

_____

_____

_____

(Example: "I'm a builder. A storyteller. A creator who turns pain into purpose and vision into reality.")

This is what I'm building:

Be bold. This isn't about what's "realistic." This is about what's *true*.

_____

_____

_____

(Example: "I'm building a global brand that empowers authors to become icons and lead movements.")

This is the life I'm creating:

Not just business. What do your mornings look like? Where do you live? Who's around you? How does it feel to wake up in your world?

_____

_____

_____

(Example: "Freedom. I wake up with peace. I lead with purpose. I work with fire. I'm surrounded by people who believe in the mission.")

This is what I'm no longer available for:

Draw the line. The jungle is full of distractions. This is your boundary.

_____

_____

_____

(Example: "I'm no longer available for self-doubt, low standards, time-wasters, or begging for approval.")

Once you fill this out, **print it. Frame it. Save it on your lock screen.** Read it every morning until it's burned into your bones.

This is not just your affirmation—it's your *compass*. The world will try to pull you in a hundred different directions. But your job is to stay rooted in *this*.

Because when your vision is clear, you stop second-guessing. You stop negotiating with fear. You stop asking the world for permission.

You don't need the full plan. You need to *know* where you're going—and *believe* in it so fiercely that no detour, delay, or doubt can shake you. No GPS. No backseat drivers.
 Just fire in your belly and eyes on the kill.

That's the Tiger Move.

2. Act Before You're Ready

Stop waiting for the stars to align. Stop waiting for the "right time." Stop waiting to feel confident.

Confidence doesn't come before the move. It comes after.

That's the lie most entrepreneurs fall for—they think they need more preparation. More credentials. More money. More followers. More certainty. But the truth? Most of the people you admire didn't wait until they were ready. They *moved* before they were qualified, and that's what made them unstoppable.

The longer you wait to feel "ready," the faster your dream dies in hesitation.

Let's be real—you already know the move you've been avoiding. That one bold action sitting in your gut like a boulder. The one that keeps whispering, "It's time." The one that scares the hell out of you because you *know* it would change everything.

That's the move. That's the thing you do in the next 72 hours.

Not next week.

Not when your website is done.

Not when your logo is perfect.

Not after you take another course.

In the next 72 hours, you take the leap.

Choose ONE of these—and *do it*:

- Launch the podcast you've been overthinking for six months.
- Send the pitch email to the media outlet or investor.
- Book the venue for the workshop or event you've dreamed of hosting.
- Offer the product—even if it's messy.
- Film the damn video—no script, no perfect lighting, just heart.
- Tell your story on social media. Raw. Real. Relatable.

You don't need permission. You don't need polish. You need *motion*.

And when you move, things move.

Here's what happens when you act before you're ready:

- People start paying attention.

- Opportunities start opening.

- Fear starts shrinking.

- Confidence starts growing.

Because confidence doesn't come from studying. It comes from *stacking reps*. From doing the thing scared. From proving to yourself that you're the kind of person who follows through.

So, here's your challenge:

In the next 72 hours, take bold, public action.

No silent planning. No secret journaling. Make a move the world can see—and let it *scare* you a little.

You'll never be "ready." But you are more than capable.

And remember: tigers don't wait to feel brave. They *strike*— and trust their power in motion.

3. Build Your Platform, Not Just Your Product

Here's the truth most entrepreneurs miss: **The product is not the power. The platform is.**

You can have the best book, course, coaching, offer—whatever. But if no one sees it, it dies in silence.

Visibility is the game. And the fastest way to get seen? **Build your own stage.**

Stop waiting for Forbes to call.

Stop begging podcasts to feature you.

Stop refreshing your inbox for someone to *pick you.*

Pick yourself.

You don't need a gatekeeper. You need a *mic*. You need a platform where your message can breathe, where your face shows up, and where your voice is the authority.

And guess what?
It doesn't need to be perfect. It just needs to be *real.*

Here are five Tiger Moves you can make **this week** to build your platform—starting now:

• **Start a YouTube Channel:** Use your iPhone. Don't wait for a studio. Show up, share your story, teach what you know. Consistency beats cinematography.

• **Host Interviews on Instagram Live:** Bring on people you admire. Talk about real stuff. Let your audience hear you think out loud. Build community in public.

- **Run a Free Zoom Workshop:** No fancy slides—just value. Teach what you know. Help people get a win. That's how you build trust—and turn followers into clients.

- **Write Your Manifesto:** Post it on social media. Tell the world what you stand for. Let people feel your fire. The bolder your message, the faster you attract your tribe.

- **Build a Landing Page:** It doesn't need to be fancy. Use Canva or any drag-and-drop builder. Drop in your offer, a photo, a video, or a payment button. Start simple—but *start.*

Most people build a product and wait. You? **You build a platform and *lead*.**

You don't need a publishing deal to be a bestselling author. You don't need TV to be seen. You don't need someone else's microphone.

You create your own megaphone.

This is how you turn content into currency. This is how you turn visibility into value. This is how you stop chasing—and start *attracting.*

Because platforms create movement.

Movement creates momentum.

And momentum?

That's what turns ideas into empires.

So, here's the rule: If it doesn't give you visibility, it's not your priority. If it doesn't give you leverage, it's not your move.

Go public. Go messy. Go loud.

The jungle doesn't reward perfection.

It rewards presence.

And the fastest way to become unforgettable—is to *be findable.*

4. Burn the Backup Plan

If you want to build something great, you can't keep one foot in safety. You cannot run full speed toward your vision while clinging to a backup plan. That "just in case" scenario—the resume you keep updating in the background, the fallback job you tell yourself you'll return to if this doesn't work out—it's not your safety net. It's your cage. And every time you hold onto it, you send the universe a quiet message: "I don't really believe this will work."

That kind of divided energy kills momentum. Clients feel it. Partners sense it. And worst of all? You feel it. You'll start hesitating when you should be moving. You'll delay decisions because you're waiting to see if it's "safe." But success doesn't come to those who try—it comes to those who decide. The world doesn't reward lukewarm effort. It rewards leaders who are all in.

So, be honest with yourself. What's your backup plan? What's the quiet exit strategy you keep in your back pocket? Write it down. Look it in the face. Then destroy it. Rip it up. Burn it. Shred it. Do whatever you need to do to let it go—not just physically, but emotionally, mentally, energetically. Because until you do, you'll always have one foot on the brake.

You weren't born for a soft landing. You were born to fly—or die trying. That's how real entrepreneurs move: all in, all fire, no exit. I'm not saying be reckless—I'm saying stop being divided. Go all in, not because it's easy, but because it's required. Tigers don't run with leashes. They hunt free or they don't hunt at all. This is your hunt. And safety isn't your savior —it's your sabotage.

Burn the plan. Fuel the fire. And watch what happens when there's no way out but through. Because here's the truth no one talks about: the moment you stop planning your escape is the moment you start designing your empire.

5. Follow Energy, Not Approval

Success isn't measured by how impressive your résumé looks or how many people clap for your work. It's measured by your energy. The truth is, most entrepreneurs don't burn out because they work too hard—they burn out because they work on the wrong things. They chase approval instead of alignment. They say yes to things that drain them because they're afraid to disappoint someone. But the real danger isn't disappointing others. It's abandoning yourself in the process.

If something gives you energy—follow it. If it drains you—question why it's still in your life. This is the practice of radical alignment. It's not always comfortable, but it's always clarifying. Approval is a moving target. The world will applaud you one minute and doubt you the next. But energy? Energy never lies. If something lights you up, pay attention. If something feels heavy, pay even closer attention.

For one full week, stop measuring success by your to-do list and start measuring it by your energy. At the end of each day, ask yourself: What gave me fire today? What drained me dry? Where did I feel fully alive? Where did I feel like I was just performing? Your answers will tell you everything you need to know. The goal isn't to be productive—it's to be powerful. You're not here to impress. You're here to ignite.

You don't need permission to shift. You don't need validation to pivot. If your fire is pulling you in a new direction, trust it. Because when your energy is aligned, your message becomes magnetic. You stop trying to push your way forward—and you start pulling people in. That's the path of a leader who builds with conviction. That's how movements begin. Follow your fire. Let it lead.

Because the ones who change the world aren't the ones who follow a plan. They're the ones who followed the spark—and turned it into a wildfire.

You don't need more directions. You need conviction. You don't need another map. You need to trust the fire already burning inside of you. That fire? It's not confusion—it's clarity trying to get your attention. It's your inner signal screaming, "Go now!" But too many people waste time chasing the perfect strategy, waiting for validation, or asking for permission. And by the time they finally feel "ready," the opportunity has passed, and someone else has already built the thing they were only dreaming about.

The world is full of paths designed by other people—for their vision, their comfort, their limits. But you weren't made to walk someone else's road. You were made to carve your own. You are not here to play it safe. You are not here to be small. You're here to lead, to create, to shake things up and leave claw marks in every space you touch. That vision that keeps you awake at night? Follow it. That bold idea that scares you and excites you at the same time? That's the one. That's your fire.

The truth is, you'll never be fully "ready." But readiness was never the goal—courage is. And when you finally stop hesitating, when you stop chasing a formula and start following your instinct, everything begins to shift. You stop moving like a follower and start leading like a force. That's the Tiger way. Bold. Focused. Unapologetically driven by fire.

So, let this be your moment. The moment you stop asking, "What's the right path?" and start declaring, "I'll build my own." You're not waiting anymore. You're not asking anymore.

You're not holding back. From this point forward, you don't follow the path. **You are the path.**

"The fastest way to become unforgettable—is to be findable."

\- Nim Stant

CHAPTER 15
EYES ON YOU

THE WAY YOU LEAD GIVES OTHERS THE COURAGE TO BELIEVE IN THEMSELVES

You may not see it yet—but your name is already echoing through places you haven't stepped into. People you've never met are watching your journey. Quietly. Closely. Not with judgment, but with hope. They're asking themselves: *If she can do it... maybe I can, too.*

You think you're just building a business? No. You're building belief—for everyone who comes after you. Every bold move you make, every time you rise after falling, every risk you take —it doesn't go unnoticed. The jungle is watching. And your courage is contagious.

I didn't know when I started that my kids were watching. I was just trying to survive. Trying to build something meaningful. Trying to keep going when it felt like everything was against me. But over time, I realized—I wasn't just building for me. I was building *in front* of them. They were learning how to rise because they saw me refuse to stay down.

Legacy isn't some distant event that happens when you've "made it." Legacy is right now. It's being written in how you handle pressure, how you treat people, how you keep your word. It's in the decisions you make when no one's clapping, when no one's posting about you, when no one's validating you. That's what shapes who you become—and who gets to follow after you.

Your story matters *not because it's perfect,* but because it's real. That messy chapter you want to skip over? That's someone else's survival guide. That failure you feel embarrassed by? That's the moment someone else will use as fuel. You don't need a million followers to make a generational ripple. You just need to keep moving.

So, don't shrink. Don't go quiet. Don't convince yourself that your impact is too small to matter. Because while you're wondering if you're doing enough, someone else is watching you and whispering, "Because of you, I didn't quit."

You were never just building a business.

You were building belief.

You were building culture.

You were building a legacy.

That's what tigers do. They don't move for applause. They move with intention. And when they do? The jungle shifts. The air changes. Others rise.

So, now the question becomes: What will you do with that awareness? Knowing the jungle is watching isn't about pressure—it's about purpose. It's not about performing. It's about walking with a deeper sense of responsibility. Not just for the brand you're building, but for the standard you're setting. Because every move you make—every bold decision, every quiet act of discipline, every time you rise when it would be easier to quit—you're showing others what's possible. You're not just chasing a dream. You're modeling what it looks like to lead with integrity, to move with conviction, to stay in the fight long after the crowd goes home.

Whether it's your kids watching how you handle a tough week, or a stranger scrolling past your video who sees a reflection of their own struggle in your story—you are the evidence that it can be done. You don't need a stage to make an impact. You don't need a million followers to shift the culture. You just need to keep going. Because every time you do, someone else takes one step closer to their own breakthrough.

That's what legacy really is. Not a headline. Not a trophy. But a ripple of courage that moves through people—because you moved first.

So, launch the offer. Post the video. Send the pitch. Be louder than your doubt. Move with that same fire that got you here. Because the world isn't just watching to see what you do next. The world is watching to find their own courage in your story. This isn't the end. It's the beginning of your leadership era.

And now that the fire is lit… don't dim it.

Move boldly. Speak clearly. Lead visibly.

Because the jungle is watching—and you are the one they've been waiting for.

BEFORE YOU GO... READ THIS FIRST

You've made it to the end of this book, but this isn't the end of your story—it's the beginning of your leadership era. This final moment isn't about motivation. It's about *movement*. Because none of what you just read matters unless you apply it.

The jungle doesn't reward the smartest. It rewards the bold— the ones who take action when no one's watching. The ones who decide that *their life* is the permission slip for others. If that's you—then let's do this.

Grab a pen. Get honest. Don't overthink it. This isn't about getting it "right"—it's about getting *real*. These next few prompts are meant to ignite something inside you and remind you: the world doesn't change when you *learn*. It changes when you *move*.

Let's move.

TIGER ACTION STEPS:
LEAD LIKE THE JUNGLE IS WATCHING

1. Write Your Ripple Statement

_____

_____

_____

Leadership isn't just about building something for yourself—it's about creating momentum that others can catch. The jungle moves because _you_ move. So, ask yourself:

Who are you really doing this for? Whose life could change because you kept going?

Fill in the blanks:

• "When I rise, I give permission for _____ to rise too."

• "My story will give hope to _____."

• "My business exists to impact _____."

Put this statement where you'll see it every day. Let it anchor your decisions and fuel your fire when things get hard.

2. Identify One Silent Watcher

You might not hear applause. But someone is watching you right now—quietly hoping you'll keep going. They might be your child, your client, your sister, or even a stranger online. Your courage is writing their permission slip.

Tiger Task:

- Think of one person who could be quietly observing your journey.
- Write them a short message or letter (even if you don't send it):
- "Here's what I want you to know about rising..."
- "If I can do this, you can too because..."

Doing this will shift your mindset from "I hope I'm doing enough" to "I'm already making impact."

3. Audit Your Leadership Footprint

Every day, whether you realize it or not, you're leaving footprints. You're showing people how to rise, how to handle pressure, how to move through setbacks. It's time to take inventory.

Ask yourself:

- What did I model this month through my choices?
- Did I choose integrity when no one was looking?
- Did I play small... or did I lead boldly, even without validation?

- Would I be proud if my kids/team/community followed my lead exactly?

Your leadership isn't built in the spotlight. It's built in the unseen moments. Audit them—and own them.

4. Post Your Courage

Your story has power. Not the polished version. The real one. The one with pain, grit, and lessons. Someone out there is waiting to hear it—to know they're not alone.

Tiger Challenge:

- Pick one real lesson from your life: a failure, a risk, a comeback.
- Share it publicly (Instagram, LinkedIn, Facebook, your newsletter).
- Don't share for validation. Share for *impact*. For *legacy*.

Your vulnerability might be the exact spark someone else needs to keep going.

5. Create a "Because of Me" List

It's easy to forget the ripple effect you've already made. But your presence, your work, your resilience—it's already shifted lives. Let's make it visible.

Write down 3–5 people or situations that changed because of you:

- "Because of me, [person] started their business."
- "Because of me, [person] believed in their dream again."
- "Because of me, [situation] went from stuck to rising."

Revisit this list often. Add to it as you grow. You're not just building a business. You're building belief in others—*and that's the real legacy.*

FINAL TIGER REMINDER

You don't need to wait for the world to hand you a crown. You've already earned your roar. I didn't write this book to impress you—I wrote it to remind you that you're not alone. Because I've been there too. I've been the one questioning everything, wondering if I'm doing enough, trying to be strong for everyone else while quietly falling apart. I've built things with shaky hands and no guarantees, holding onto nothing but a little bit of fire and a whole lot of faith.

If that's where you are right now—I see you. And I want you to know that just by choosing to keep going, you're already leading. Your journey might feel invisible at times. Unnoticed. Uncelebrated. But people are paying attention. Your kids. Your team. Your community. People you've never met. They're watching—not with judgment, but with hope. And every time you rise, they believe they can too.

You don't have to be loud to lead. You just have to be real. To show up with heart. To walk through the fear and keep moving anyway. That's what legacy really looks like. It's not a viral post or a moment of applause—it's who you are when no one's clapping. It's how you treat people. It's how you keep your word. It's how you move forward even when it's hard.

So, if this book gave you just one thing, let it be this: You matter. Your voice matters. Your fire matters. Every step you take forward sends a ripple, whether you see it now or not. Don't shrink. Don't go quiet. Not now. Because someone, somewhere, is watching you and whispering, "Because of you, I didn't quit."

This was never just about building a business. You've been building a legacy all along.

So, keep going. Not to prove something—but because you already are something.

A Tiger.

And Tigers move the jungle.

ABOUT THE AUTHOR
NIM STANT

Nim Stant is an entrepreneur, author, and influencer with an unwavering commitment to unlocking the full potential of the human experience. Born into a broken middle-class family, Nim learned from an early age the power of resilience, determination, and living with purpose. Her journey has been one of transformation, and she has channeled her experiences into a vibrant career dedicated to helping others break free from limiting beliefs, pursue their dreams, and take bold action in their lives.

With over twenty years of experience, Nim's passion for empowering others has only grown stronger. In 2020, she founded the International Impact Book Awards, a groundbreaking initiative that opens doors for independent authors and publishers worldwide. Through this platform, Nim has cultivated a diverse and dynamic community of literary talent, providing authors with the recognition, support, and resources they need to share their stories and expertise with the world.

Nim's work is driven by a deep-seated belief that every story has the power to change lives. She is fervently dedicated to helping authors and entrepreneurs amplify their voices, overcome obstacles, and transform their messages into movements that resonate globally. Through the International Impact Book Awards, she is on a mission to elevate the literary world and empower authors to make a meaningful impact on their audiences.

Nim has had the privilege of working with world-renowned authors and entrepreneurs such as Sharon Lechter, Mark Victor Hansen, Sean Kanan, Brian Tracy, Dr. Joe Vitale, Daymond John, Kevin Harrington, Jeff Fagin, Alex Hormozi, and many more. Her expertise and influence have been recognized globally, with features in over 480 media outlets worldwide.

In addition to her work with the International Impact Book Awards, Nim unites global thought leaders and educators to foster education, healing, and community support. Her initiatives provide a powerful platform for distributing educational content, inspiring positive change, and igniting the potential within every individual she reaches. Whether through her interviews on Global Thought Leaders TV, her bestselling book *Go All In*, or her engaging talks at renowned events like TEDx, Nim's work is infused with a passion for guiding others to live their lives with full intention and purpose.

Nim's heart for service extends beyond her professional endeavors. She is deeply involved in philanthropy, partnering with organizations like "Be Good, Do Good, Spread Good" and founding the "Promise From Above" non-profit. Through these efforts, she has spearheaded numerous community projects in Thailand, providing essential school supplies and support to underprivileged children. Nim Stant's life and work are a vibrant expression of her passion for empowering others, her dedication to creating positive change, and her relentless pursuit of excellence. She is a beacon of inspiration for authors, entrepreneurs, and anyone striving to make a lasting impact on the world.

NimStant.com

www.ingramcontent.com/pod-product-compliance
Lightning Source LLC
Chambersburg PA
CBHW050446150626
46551CB00029B/1829